PRICING STRATEGY

An Interdisciplinary Approach

PRICING STRATEGY

An Interdisciplinary Approach

by Morris Engelson

First edition published 1995.

Published and distributed by:

> Joint Management Strategy
> P.O. Box 25170
> Portland, OR 97225

Printed and bound in the United States of America.

Standard Book Number: 0-9642870-6-4

Library of Congress Catalog Number: 94-78087

Publisher's Cataloging in Publication
(Prepared by Quality Books Inc.)

Engelson, Morris.
   Pricing strategy: an interdisciplinary approach / by Morris Engelson.
   p. cm.
   Includes bibliographical references and index.
   ISBN 0-9642870-6-4

   1. Pricing.   I. Title.

HF5416.5.E64 1995   338.5'2'01
                                                QBI94-21285

With thanks to the
Source of all Inspiration.

Dedicated to my children:

You are the future,
unlike the content of this book
which merely plans for it.

Foreword

I would like to start with a few words about what this book is about, and especially what it's not about. There's a rule somewhere that authors of technical or educational works should not communicate in the first person. This rule was broken, as you can see, by the first word in the first sentence. The fact is, that the ideas presented here don't come from a secret source of wisdom. These are the ideas, suggestions, and most of all opinions of an individual. Hopefully, more than three decades in the workplace in a variety of job functions, coupled with study has yielded some useful ideas. But that's all it is — ideas and opinions. I have no computer link to revealed truth. This is especially so when dealing with future planning, and particularly someone else's future. It's said that those who trust a crystal ball are doomed to eat ground glass. It's your job. I would not presume to tell you how to do it. Find in this book what fits and makes sense to you. Ignore the rest. Ideally, we would sit down together and talk. Exchange ideas. However, that's not possible. But an informal, conversational style might help.

Another break from tradition is the avoidance of footnotes or references. People don't talk in footnotes. That doesn't mean that I'm presenting original discoveries. Chances are that everything I have to say has an origin in something I've read or heard. I don't know how many books and articles related to our subject I've read over the years. Almost as difficult would be to construct a list of topics from formal courses and informal seminars. I know that I have referred to about one hundred books and articles in preparing this manuscript. These, and other materials, could be cross referenced. However, what would be gained in further study possibilities would be lost in ease of comprehension. I've opted instead for a less rigorous style. It goes without saying that I'm fully responsible for the content, regardless of where the ideas come from. Errors in logic or information are fully the responsibility of the author.

Thinking about this book, I'm reminded of a phrase much used by a practical-minded teacher in a business course I attended — "so what, and who cares?" Here we have one more version on how to succeed in business — so what, and who cares? Don't we have enough business books already? The truth is that I can not offer any assurances that this book will do you good. I do feel fairly comfortable though, that it will not cause any harm. I would be very pleased if you should find my writing sufficiently compelling to convince you to try some of the procedures described here. But the emphasis should be on "try", and not on "must". Remember to only try, and stop if it doesn't feel right.

Another answer to, "so what, and who cares?" is that this book is different. Not better, necessarily, but certainly different. It's different both in focus and in treatment. The focus is on pricing as a unifying theme across all business functions. Strategy, marketing, finance, etc. are taken as supporting elements for a business-winning price, rather than the more common procedure where strategy, or whatever, is the driver and price a supporting element.

The treatment is different because it looks to the interface between operational functions. This is a result of the business situations that this author experienced over the last 30 years. My first serious business lesson occurred in 1964 when, as the engineering VP of a small start-up, I was to discuss the possible acquisition of our company by a much larger corporation. We were successful by every measure I could think of. Sales growth was at an annualized rate of several hundred percent, and profit was very good. Imagine my surprise that there was not enough cash to pay for my airfare. That's when I first discovered the difference between profits and cash flow, and the relationship between orders/sales growth and cash use. As a scientist, I had not considered such things before, but once discovered it was fascinating. Since that time, I've been responsible for technical and business management involving strategy, marketing, and general management on a global scale, have attended numerous seminars and courses in marketing, strategy, finance, management..., but the shock of that first lesson is still with me.

We had to sell our company because we were too successful and literally ran out of money. What would have happened, I wonder, if I and my other functional counterparts understood then some of the seemingly simple and basic relationships that I understand now? Perhaps nothing would change, but it would be by choice and not by necessity. Was the business as successful as I thought, or should I have used a different criterion of success? Were my ideas about success different from our marketing manager? Should the engineering manager look at success in a different light than marketing, or manufacturing or finance? Is there some unifying way for all the different functional entities in a business to consider success and failure? My answer: look at the most basic, most essential element that no business can do without. My choice — pricing. The result is this book. I hope you enjoy reading and using it as much as I enjoyed writing it.

Table of Contents

Chapter 4 — Introduction To Strategic Behavior

Chapter 5 — Pricing Analysis and Planning

Chapter 6 — Supplementary Material

Chapter 7 — Appendix

Chapter 1
Introduction

1.1 Pricing as bridge

Does this situation appear a bit familiar?

- The Marketing Communications manager is a genius. Response to promotions is the best you ever had. Too bad potential customers are more interested in the advertising than the product.

- You have a whiz in manufacturing. The output rate is way above what anybody could do before. Too bad your warehouse is full of inventory that nobody wants.

- Your financial manager is amazing. Imagine being able to determine an internal rate of return without a calculator. Too bad that the only advice this person knows is, "increase the price, we need more profit."

- Your marketing manager is a jewel. Orders are up by 50%. Too bad the products have no margin, and manufacturing doesn't know how to build the stuff.

A business manager usually identifies with some particular function, or functional objective(s). The manufacturing manager is supposed to know something about building products. The Marketing communications manager is concerned about promoting these products and getting leads for Sales to follow up. The financial manager looks at cash flow, return on assets or tax rates. The business will not succeed without proper attention to these areas. But, the business will not succeed if attention is placed only on these areas. *The ultimate objective of every business manager, no matter what the function or management designation, should be to aim for overall business success.*

This is what this book is about — business success. It doesn't matter what you consider as success for your business — profit, sales growth, return on investment — this book considers its implications, relationship to other measures, and how to get desired results. The common theme that holds everything together is the pricing decision. That is because ultimately, to be in business, you need to sell something. The price forms the bridge between you and the buyer, and between profit or loss.

All businesses can benefit from this material. However, the emphasis is on manufacturing rather than service organizations. Likewise, all managerial/supervisory personnel will find the book useful. The emphasis, however, is on small business function operating managers and functional managers such as sales, finance, manufacturing, human resources, etc. These people, directly on the firing line, so to speak, have the best opportunity to immediately start gaining results from this material.

This book is structured along two ideas. One is that if you carefully consider price, you will in the process consider all essential elements of the business. The other idea is that while effective organizational functions such as sales, or finance, or manufacturing are individually vital to business health, it's in the interface between these that the margin between success and the also-rans resides. Using these ideas will not make you successful overnight. And it is no substitute for everything else that needs to be done. It will not resurrect an enterprise already half in the grave. That may require drastic surgery, if it can be done at all. Rather, the intent is to make the moderately ill better. When combined with other treatments, it can make the ill well. Ultimately, we would like to make the well stronger and more resistant to future problems. The essential objective is to strengthen the interfaces so that each functional group becomes more efficient in carrying out its function, and also more effective in working with the other functions to achieve the joint objectives of the overall business. The basis for this idea is very simple. Consider:

It seems strange that an individual working alone can frequently accomplish so much more than when working with others. We all know of individuals working alone, or with just a few other people, who succeed in creating a new business out of nothing. Then, as soon as the organization gets larger, everything falls apart. Is it just a matter of accident or luck? Could it be that these very smart, competent, and hard working people suddenly become stupid, incompetent, and lazy? Of course not. We still have the same person with the same degree of ability or lack of it. The person is the same. But the external environment is not the same. Now there are many people to interface and coordinate with and, more importantly, these are within diverse operating and functional groups. All of these people and groups could be doing a superb job, but not necessarily the same job. It does the team (read business) no good to have one of its best runners, efficiently running in the wrong direction. Results would be better if this person didn't run at all.

This situation is usually described on the basis of stages in organizational evolution. The start-up with just a handful of people is different from a fully operating business involving fifty people. A single location $50 million business is different from a multi-plant, global $500 million enterprise. We talk about different organizational structures, and the need for the structure to fit the life-cycle position of the business. We talk about the needed difference in mental outlook between a single individual entrepreneur starting a business and the president, leader, of a global enterprise. All of these, and other, descriptions result from a single factor.

Communication and understanding between people is flawed. It's never perfect. No one can crawl into someone else's mind and know all that that person knows, or feel what that person feels. Imperfect communication and understanding leads to imperfect execution of effort even when all parties are willing, or even eager, to cooperate. Both the efficiency of understanding (agreement on both goals and procedures), and efficiency of execution (i.e., doing something and getting results) are important in getting desired results in a group environment.

Clearly, a 100% preoccupation with understanding is not desirable because eventually someone must do something. Similarly, all doing and no understanding is equally bad since wrong action can be worse than no action. One answer is to give everybody a stake in an essential business decision that is affected by all functional groups.

My choice for this, bridging, function is price. Looking at the price ensures that each functional grouping will have an appreciation for the needs, procedures, and contribution of other functions. Marketing, for instance, needs to appreciate that a 1% reduction in manufacturing cost can be worth as much as two or more percent customer price change, which can be worth several percent of market share, which may mean more income/profits, hence more investment in manufacturing productivity, which leads to lower manufacturing cost, which, etc. The business wins, and specifically marketing wins in its mission to gain more customers. Likewise, manufacturing needs to understand that building two more model numbers will double sales volume, this will improve profits even though it costs more, it will provide more volume and jobs for manufacturing, etc. Again, not only does the business win, but manufacturing wins.

There's nothing really new here. On-the-job training has been around a long time. What is different is the perspective. The idea is not to teach marketing to a marketing person. Certainly, some of that is involved, but it's not the main thrust. The idea is to teach marketing disciplines, say positioning or pricing strategy, to the non-marketing functions; to teach manufacturing economics to the marketing people; to teach business strategy to everyone, etc. Furthermore, it's not the intention to provide this cross-disciplinary training as a watered-down version of what the discipline practitioners get. In other words, it's not the intention to turn the scientists into junior marketers. A junior marketeer usually has good depth in a small area, and the breadth increases as the junior becomes a senior. But, the scientists are not looking to become marketing gurus, whether junior or senior. Rather, the full breadth of the discipline must be maintained but explained in a way that shows how other functions fit in and contribute to the whole.

Naturally, an enterprise needs strong and competent professionals in all disciplines. Financial people must understand business finance issues. They also must understand how manufacturing or marketing or whoever fits into the whole and contributes to the whole. They must also understand how the various groupings and functions fit together to help each other and the overall business. Thus the barriers at the functional interfaces to doing the right thing and doing the thing right are significantly reduced. The direction taken is a shorter path to the objective, and the efficiency of travelling the road is improved. Any decent organization has good people, good operational functions and a workable organization structure. These must be constantly examined and improved. But that is not enough. The difference between good and championship quality is in the interface between functions. That is where those who have a chance to win actually win or lose.

Unfortunately, inter-functional understanding is not easy. Most people are familiar with some version of this story. An engineer, a sociologist, and a statistician applied for a job. The interview consisted of just one question — how much is one plus one. The engineer took out a calculator, keyed in the problem, and said that one plus one equals two to eight decimal places. He would need access to a more powerful calculator to get a more accurate answer. The sociologist promised to bring back the answer in one week, after a representative population group was interviewed. The statistician responded with, "what answer would you like to have?". The underlying assumption upon which much of this book is based is that price is the integrating idea that will lead to coherent behavior between functions. Hence the subtitle, "an interdisciplinary approach".

The material is presented in seven chapters. The first is an **introduction** to the purpose, content and how to best use the material in this book. The second chapter explains **pricing concepts. Pricing procedures,** including more advanced concepts will be found in the third chapter. The concept of **strategic behavior**, including a refresher on strategic planning, is presented in chapter four. You will find questions, prompts, outlines, and procedures for **price analysis and planning** in chapter five. The **supplementary material** in chapter six consists of advanced, or controversial, or esoteric concepts that will be of interest to some, but not to all readers of this book. The final chapter, titled **appendix,** contains some new material, but mostly a repetition of graphs, tables, and analysis forms presented previously. These are materials that you will find useful as you work on your own, unique pricing issues.

1.2 "A penny for your thoughts"

A penny was once worth a great deal. Still, I wonder how many thoughts, and what sort of thoughts, one could buy for a penny, even a hundred years ago? Today the penny is not worth much. Yet, how many thoughts do you know that you would not take even if someone paid you? The fact is that not all thoughts are equal, neither are all pennies, or for that matter not all needs either. The thoughts of an attorney can be worth many pennies if you are accused of a crime, and at the same time worthless to others. Not only intangibles like thoughts, but physical items such as shoes, computers, or tables also differ as to worth and value. Nevertheless, someone somehow arrives at a "price" for each of these. Who should set the price? On what basis, or in what manner should the price be set? What is the best price? What does "best" mean in this context?

Price, sale, worth, value. Setting a price, just any price, is easy. It doesn't take much effort to just state a number. Unfortunately, it's only when someone is willing to pay the price that the price has any value. Finding a buyer may not indicate that you have set the best, or even a good price. Inability to sell at your price does indicate, however, that you have set a useless price. Here is how my dictionary puts it. "Price: value, worth, the amount of one thing that is exchanged in sale for another."

There's an exchange based on the value, or worth, of the item to be sold. Money, the penny in the quotation, is the exchange medium through which the value is established. If the penny is worth less, as it is today compared to ten years ago, then it takes more pennies to acquire a fixed-value item. If one item is worth less than another item, then it takes fewer pennies to buy this item. That seems simple enough. Just set the price equal to the value.

But who decides on the value? Is it the buyer, or is it the seller? The seller might, for instance, establish a value based on expenses. But this could be totally at variance with the buyer's expectations. Furthermore, what does the word "price" really mean? To the seller it usually means the pennies received for the item. Price to the buyer, though, could include the cost of using, installing and servicing the item. If value to the seller is based on, or at least includes, costs, then we have to consider where the costs come from. Do we include the cost of making the item, of selling the item, or of designing the item? Should all of these costs assume equal importance? Who is the seller? Is it the salesperson in the store, the marketing strategist, the person who builds it, the person who designed it, the business proprietor or manager?

Who should be responsible for setting the selling price? The selling price is usually set by one function, such as marketing, or one person, such as the organization manager. Nevertheless, all areas of the business enterprise contribute to the decision, whether they know it or not. No business can long endure if prices are well below cost. The manufacturing function contributes to the pricing decision to the degree that high manufacturing costs force prices above the level of the buyer's valuation, or below the level where the business can make a profit. Sales will not occur if the selling function is not able to show the buyer that reduced installation costs represent a better value or price, etc. Thus, all business functions are critically involved in the pricing decision, though only one function may be responsible for it. All business functions must be, at least, aware of their impact on product pricing decisions. Discussion of the concept of customer value, the concept of business profit and the impact on, and contribution to, of the various business functions follows.

What is value? Value is affected by three sources: the user/buyer, the seller, and competing sellers. Each contributes to the notion of value.

Certainly, the buyer is a primary, if not the primary, contributor. The buyer ultimately decides whether to buy or not to buy the item. The final determination of value is in the mind of the buyer. But the buyer does not make the decision in isolation. I well remember when a price of more than 70¢ per gallon of gasoline was a ridiculously poor value. Suddenly, a short time later, anything under a dollar was a bargain. The buyer still decided on what is a good value, but the external signals had changed. The signals come from you, the seller, and from other competing sellers. The buyer's notions of value can be influenced. You, the seller, need to ensure that your product is priced in a way that represents good value to the buyer. That's elementary logic. But you must go beyond that. Good pricing aims at enhancing the worth of the product so that the value is increased regardless of the price.

Most people are familiar with some variation of the following story:

A carpet store owner acquired some very fine carpets, which he was unable to sell no matter what he did. He finally decided on a 50% sale, instructed his assistant to change the price by two, then left town. All the carpets were sold when he returned, but not at half the original price but at double the original price.

The misunderstanding by the assistant totally changed the pricing parameters. The original price was too much for the normal store clients. They could not afford to buy carpets at that price no matter how great a bargain. But the price was too low to attract the people who were interested in the very finest merchandise. An increase in price brought in people who could afford the price, appreciate the quality of the carpets, and were actually intending to buy something.

The buyer. A want or need or desire for the product, knowledge and appreciation of the value of the product, and financial ability to pay for the product, describes a desirable customer. Pricing a product properly requires that you decide on an intended buyer, and you understand this buyer. The very high price carpet buyer, in the story, is a totally different type of person than a low price carpet buyer. Clearly, the carpet store was not used to dealing with this type of buyer. The worth of the merchandise fit this type of buyer, but the store owner set a price which fit a different sort of merchandise. The disparity between the worth and the price made the sale difficult. Too low a price in relation to the worth is almost as bad for getting a sale, as too high a price. Certainly too low a price is very bad as far as profitability is concerned. Therefore, you must know who the intended buyer is, and assure that product worth and price are properly aligned to fit the target buyer.

A buyer wants to get the highest value purchase. Usually, that means lowest cost. What, however, is the cost to the buyer? Cost to the buyer is not necessarily the same as the price of the product. Imagine that you are selling flooring products for new housing. The building contractor is the buyer. This buyer doesn't personally use your item. The flooring is sold to someone else, after installation in a house. What's the cost to the buyer? It's the price of your material plus installation. Therefore, you can charge more than others if the installation time for your material is less. The lesson is that selling price is an important, but not the only, contributor to buyer cost. To fully understand the value of your product you must understand the business of the buyer. The house builder values a low installation time. It's part of the cost. A do-it-yourselfer, however, may not care. What's an extra hour of personal time compared to greater out of pocket expense? Furthermore, since the purchase decision ultimately depends on the value perceived by the buyer, it's important that the buyer know about the value ingredients of your product. Minimum installation time will not sell your flooring if the house builder doesn't know about it.

The buyer's condition at the moment affects the pricing possibilities. The value of a bottle of water is very much different to the same person walking in the desert versus swimming in a lake. I would pay a great deal for a drink of water if lost in the desert. But, how I felt about it, and behaved toward the buyer in the future, would depend on the price. The worth is there. The water saved my life, and my life is worth a great deal to me. Nevertheless, just because the buyer will agree on the worth doesn't mean that the buyer considers it fair. Don't expect this buyer to do business with you in the future when there are other alternatives. Therefore, you must consider the impact of the pricing decision on the future as well as the present. You must also consider the effect of competitors, both current and future.

The competition. Pricing decisions would be much easier if there were no competition. Usually, though, there's competition for the same or similar item or some other item that will do the same job. A drink of water in the desert may be worth to me everything I have, unless I'm in a city in the desert. Then I'll refuse to pay more than what the nearest grocery store will charge. Competitor prices help establish a value position in the mind of the buyer. This places an upper bound on what you can charge. That's bad enough. Worse yet is the impact on the future, and ability to make rational plans. Competition makes for uncertainty. A competitor can change prices and/or value impacting product features. This means that you must always be prepared to change your pricing position. There's no such thing as a permanent price. You must also be prepared to change the value components of your product. There's no such thing as a permanent product. This uncertainty affects your need for profit. The more uncertain the future, the more you need to be prepared to live through difficult financial times. Even worse than tough competitors that do a good job, are inept competitors that do a poor job. A competitor that does not understand pricing can be a disaster for everybody by establishing a totally unrealistic product value in the mind of the buyer. No pricing analysis is complete without taking into account the current competitive situation, and expectation of future competitor behavior.

The seller. You are the seller. Surely you ought to know what you're doing now, what you intend to do in the future, what you want to accomplish, what your pricing objectives are, what the value ingredients of your product are, etc. Sadly, many people don't know many of these things. You're the seller. It's your choice what to tell the buyer about your product. Do you want to emphasize installation time, initial price, choice of colors, dirt resistance, or what? Would you prefer that your competitor explain what your product is about? This is your chance to enhance the value in the perception of the buyer. This is also your chance to differentiate yourself, to be different, from the competitor's products. The more you're different, the less you're at the mercy of what the competitors will do in the future. It pays to be different even if your competitors behave rationally. A commodity item, essentially identical to other items, can only compete on price. The power of the buyer to control your prices is strong when all you have to offer is a lower price. Still, a commodity may be exactly what you want it to be if you happen to have the lowest manufacturing cost. Then your competitors would be at a disadvantage if you could force them to also behave as commodities. The key is not what price you choose, but how and why you do it. Choice of a commodity position implies something totally different about your manufacturing expertise than being the highest performance and service provider. Whatever you choose, it must be part of a coherent and integrated plan that takes into account all of your business functions, as well as the buyer and the competitors.

Profit. The notion of profit is not a simple idea. There are many diverse aspects to profit. It's difficult to balance the need or desire for various "profits". Furthermore, how profit is used, and why profit is needed is frequently misunderstood. Many people equate profit with greed, something to be tolerated but not admired. Some people have the idea that profit is something the manager, or owner, takes home every night to put under the mattress. Not so. Profit is a necessary, absolutely critical, ingredient for an organization to stay in business in our free enterprise system. In its simplest form, profit is an indicator of how well the business is performing, a feedback mechanism to correct and improve performance. On a more fundamental basis, however, profit is the insurance to ensure survival in an uncertain future, it's the investment capital for future expansion of jobs or new machinery to improve productivity, it pays the taxes to run schools and build roads. Private people call it savings, that which is left over from earnings after on-going expenses. Without savings there's no new car, no college for junior, no hospitalization for an unexpected illness, and no possibility of starting your own business. There's, no doubt, such a thing as greed and fraud in business, but that shouldn't be confused with the notion of operating profit.

Here's a well known story:

A very successful business owner, who failed finance 101 in school, was asked for the secret of his success. "I just follow what I learned in school", he said. "I buy merchandise at $1 and sell at $2. It's amazing what a 1% markup will do for you."

Profit results when the selling price exceeds expenses. The greater the difference the greater the profit. The owner, in our story, would never have charged a 100% premium had he realized that that is what doubling the cost represents. He thought it was just a modest 1% profit. Would a real 1% profit have kept him in business? It depends. A single percent per year on the cost of the merchandise will hardly cover the telephone bills, let alone cost of stocking and reselling the goods. If new goods, however, come in and get sold on a weekly basis, then we have a very substantial return of over 50% per year!

Clearly, proper pricing involves matching price to buyer value. Your cost is not involved in this. Just because you have a high cost doesn't mean that others will pay a high price. Cost is nevertheless a factor, because you must end with a profit. Computation of profit and deciding how much is an acceptable minimum is not a simple matter. The matter of a minimum is particularly important, because a business will not stay in business long unless minimum profit needs are met. This means the necessary minimum for the whole business. And since some areas might lose money, now and then, the other areas need to actually deliver more than the minimum.

Price, demand, and profit. The carpet story not withstanding, usually the lower the price the more units sold. The price-demand curve shows how unit sales relate to price per unit. The basic graph is an exponential, going asymptotic to both unit price and volume quantity. Presumably, in a very large population, somebody could be found who will be willing to pay a very high price. Similarly, it's assumed that most people will get one of the items if the price is sufficiently low. This is why the price-demand relationship is asymptotic in both directions. Whether the theory is correct or not doesn't really matter, because the extreme points are not viable positions. The high price, low volume area provides enormous price per unit. Too bad that total sales revenue is not enough to support a business. On the other end, more volume means more losses if you cannot cover per unit costs. But this leaves plenty of maneuvering room in the middle. The question is what's the objective?

A maximum sales revenue objective provides an easily calculated price. It's a simple mathematical exercise to compute the unit price which, when multiplied by units volume, yields the maximum sales revenue.

No, you say. That's not my objective. I would like to maximize units volume so as to keep most customers away from the competition. But I'm not willing to let sales revenue go down by more than 5%. A simple calculation provides a price. Forget it! That's not what we're after. What we really want is to get the highest price per unit possible, consistent with no more than a 5% revenue loss. Yes, the calculation can be easily made. Well, forget all this revenue stuff. We really want to maximize profits by deducting cost from revenue. That too can be easily calculated.

All of the above, and many other items, are easily calculated from the price-demand numbers. General formulas relating price, cost, revenue, units, profit, etc. permit strategic comparison analyses without regard to specific values. Thus, it can be shown, for instance, that adding the full cost to the maximum revenue price will not maximize profits. Adding half the cost is a closer approximation. For example, the manufacturing cost of your product is 10 monetary units each. Based on customer and market analysis you estimate a certain price-demand relationship such as 20 units, or 20,000 units if you wish, will be sold at a price of 30 per unit, etc. This leads to the following results:

price	60	35	32	31	30	26	25	24	20	10	5
units	3	16	18.3[1]	19.3	20	24	25	26	30	42	55
revenue	180	560	586	598	600	624	625	624	600	420	275
P-C	50	25	22	21	20	16	15	14	10	0	-5
profit	150	400	403	405	400	384	375	364	300	0	-275

We note that the maximum sales revenue occurs at a price of 25 per unit. We can gain 20% more units (30 / 25) for only a 4% (600 / 625) loss in sales revenue. This may be a good pricing decision if we plan to introduce a follow-on product in the future that we hope to sell to currently happy customers. We note also that a 4 percent drop in revenue will increase profits by 6.7% (400 / 375) by going to a price of 30. This would be a wise decision if the profit level were very important, even though we want to maximize sales revenue.

Speaking of profit, let's examine the decision to increase unit volume. It's true that revenue doesn't change much as the price goes from 25 to 20. Total profit, however, goes from 375 down to 300. Do we still want to do it? What if our primary objective is to maximize profits? Here the best price is 31, just over half the cost more than the maximum revenue price of 25. The increment would be exactly half the cost if the price-demand relationship were linear.

What's the cost? Many other, less obvious, considerations are helped by analyzing the price-demand relationship. Look at the profit. It changes just over 1% from the optimum price of 31 to a higher price of 35. The profit does not change much, but unit volume drops by 20%, from 19.3 to 16. We know that there are many other costs in operating a business than just the cost of the item to be sold. Many of these costs such as stocking, transportation, sales commission, after sale repairs, order processing, answering customer inquiries… are a function of sales volume. By operating our business at a lower volume we might actually gain back more savings than we lose in direct product profit. In fact, what we called profit is not really profit at all.

---

[1] No, there's no sale of 18.3 fractional units. In real life, we have 18 units at a price just above 32. But the mathematics work just as well both ways. I did it this way to permit specific-number revenue and profit values for comparison.

Building a product is not all there is to a business. There are many other functions and costs. Some of these costs are enumerated above, but there are many more. Some of these costs are related to an individual product. Shipping the product, servicing the product after sale, advertising the product are such costs. Other costs are not related to a specific product, at all. Research to develop new products, the cost to operate a payroll function, painting the building, maintaining stockholder records are part of an on-going business, yet we cannot say that these are related to a specific product. Some costs are related to a specific product but not really to its volume. Tools and machinery unique to the manufacture of a product must be acquired no matter what the sales volume. These non-volume, and non-product related costs can be much greater than the actual manufacturing cost. Here the mathematics of capacity utilization gets into the act. Is the plant outputting as much as it can or is it half idle? The marketing oriented person, who is usually responsible for pricing, may not think about that. Yet, the impact on results can be significant. This is not just financial results but also sales results and marketing strategy. Maybe the need is to go for a lower volume because non-manufacturing product related expenses are very high. Conversely, it may be critical to maintain volume because of a high break-even point due to fixed capacity costs. Clearly, sales behavior and marketing strategy will be different for the two examples.

Do you price all sales equally, or do you follow an incremental sales philosophy? Perhaps your business is such that everybody knows everybody else. Everybody knows what's going on and what the prices are. An appearance of fairness and equal treatment is critical. Then incremental pricing is probably not appropriate. However, if industry behavior is to bid, negotiate, and adjust prices at will, then incremental pricing should be considered. A high fixed cost puts a premium on volume, and a small additional volume increment can make a big difference to profits. Thus, if your product related costs are 20 per unit, your fixed costs are 100,000 and you sell units at 60, you have to sell 2,500 units at 150,000 to break even [(60 − 20) * (2500) = 100,000]. If your plant capacity is 3,000 and you are unable to find any more buyers at 60, then you would be better off by selling the excess increment at less than 60 rather than not sell at all. Incremental pricing involves not just a financial or marketing decision, it's a business strategy decision.

Remember the competition. You can get into pricing difficulties even if you do all the foregoing perfectly. You know exactly what users value, you have determined the precise impact of price on volume, you've set the price to optimize whatever the business objective calls for. All this work can be spoiled by an unexpected move from the competition. The price-demand analysis is based on the assumption of some particular competitor position for price and performance. A change in competitive product price will change your sales volume even if the price-demand relationship doesn't change. As a minimum, you'll have to make an adjustment in price, or product performance/worth or volume. But it can be worse than that. What if your competitor introduces three new products at differing price/performance ratios? This will likely change the price-demand curve, and obsolete your whole analysis.

Usually, products with significantly different price/performance ratios don't fall on the same price-demand curve, but on different ones in a family of curves. Solid silver tableware doesn't compete with the plastic type even though these are used for the same function and carry the same names — knives and forks. Where do you put the stainless steel variety? Deciding what products you compete with, and which price-demand curve you belong to, is a critical business decision. It's not just a matter of computing the right price. A right price in the wrong competitor and customer mix can mean trouble. Remember the story about the carpets? The carpets belonged on the luxury carpet curve, not the everyday carpet curve. What looked like an impossibly high price on the everyday curve, was very reasonable on the luxury one.

Unexpected moves by your competitors can destroy all of your carefully developed plans. One message, here, might be that it doesn't pay to spend too much effort on plans (more on that later). Another message is that what they can do to you, you can also do to them. Take note of competitive offerings on both your own product's demand curve, and all the other alternate curves. This requires careful consideration of what business you're in. If you're in the carpet business then you'll want to consider your everyday variety competitors, your luxury alternatives, etc. If, however, you are in the floor covering business, then you need to look at many other materials besides carpets. Are you after volume? Perhaps a change in price could gain for you against a higher cost/price carpet competitor. Perhaps the volume for alternate products, say tiles, is much larger than for your carpets. Possibly price is not the issue but rather the perceived value and objectives in the mind of the users. Perhaps you should actually increase the price but advertise in a different manner. Perhaps you should join forces with other (competitor) carpet sellers to promote carpet versus tile. Perhaps this or perhaps that. The point is that you have many more options than just dropping your price in order to increase volume.

The power of savings. Profit is what's left over after you've covered your expenses. Therefore, savings in costs flow directly into profits. It would seem that an increase in prices would do the same for you. But it's not the same. Suppose we were operating at a price of 25 in the previous price-demand example. Revenue is 625 and the gross profit is 375, or 60%. A cost saving of one unit doesn't change the revenue, but profit improves to 400, or 64%. No change in cost but a price increase from 25 to 26, yields 624 in revenue and 384 in gross profit, at 62%. The cost saving provides both better absolute profit and improved percent of sales profit. We might choose to pass our cost savings on to the customer. Then the price would come down to 24 with 624 in sales revenue. Gross profit per unit will be 15 for an overall profit of 390, at 63%. Unit volume is better than before, total profit is better than before, and percent profit is better than before we had the savings. You can see that cost savings is a much more flexible and powerful profit enhancer than a price change.

A different sort of profit enhancer, that doesn't call for a price change, is to improve perceived value. The usual procedure is to use advertising to convince the user that the product is better, or more desirable, than previously considered. That's not the only method available, or always the best method. Faster, easier, or better performance, more durability or whatever, if valued by the user, will change the price-demand relationship in your favor. You will get higher unit demand at the same price or you can charge a higher price at the same volume. Your profits will improve either way. Of course, it may call for more costs to do this. But the improved profits may be worth it. You may want to do it even at a higher cost level because of competitive considerations. It's much better that you do it to yourself before your competitor does it to you. You should also consider the impact on the competitor who may not be able to follow, and abandon the business altogether.

Whoever is setting the price needs to consider the other business functions — finance, manufacturing, research, transportation… in choosing a pricing strategy and, ultimately, a price. A slight change in one of these areas may have a greater impact than anything else. The pricing decision is part of a strategy, and the strategy involves the whole business.

Uncertainty. Your competition can do something deliberately, or accidentally to upset all your plans. A change in political orientation, a war, or an earthquake can drastically increase or restrict the flow of certain materials. Someone once said that the future is hard to predict because it hasn't happened yet. This means that your plans may not work no matter how perfect your planning and how accurate your current information. Furthermore, your current information isn't at all accurate. At best, a price-demand curve is a crude approximation to a theoretical construct. In theory, it's possible to gather all sorts of data and perform all sorts of experiments. The cost and time can be high, and the future is always uncertain. Perfection is not a major concern; avoidance of failure is. Flexibility, to change your behavior to fit results, is much more important than finding the optimum price to three decimal places. There will always be mistakes. The key is in how fast you can correct things, and survive in the meantime. This is one reason why profits need to exceed current needs. You'll need the excess next time you make a mistake.

Just because the accuracy is poor, however, doesn't mean that mathematical and financial analysis is to be ignored. On the contrary. The more you investigate the better both your strategy, and the implementation. Price-volume relationships, costs, profits, incremental profits, return on investment, payback period, break even point, capacity utilization, competitive products, alternate product substitutes, expense breakdown by fixed and variable and by product and non-product related, user/buyer needs wants and segments… are all constituent elements to the pricing decision. Availability of back up contingency plans, understanding in all business functions of their impact on profits and pricing, should be part of the pricing decision.

Pricing decisions are sometimes made in a hurry, or as an afterthought or handed to an inexperienced junior member of a junior department. That can be costly! The pricing decision is one of the most critical in running a business. Once made and implemented, it's not easily changed. Remember that everything in your business is an expense except the sale of something. The price is a critical ingredient in whether sales will, or will not, come in. The difference between a proper and improper price can be the difference between success and failure for the entire business.

Chapter 2
Pricing Concepts

2.1 A word about process

Most of this section consists of questions, rather than instructional answers. The reason is that the questions are universal, but the answers are particular. This is your job, your business and your life. You should decide on what to do based on your beliefs and your answers. No outsider will know as much about your business as you do, and chances are that you'll make good decisions provided you answer the right questions.

But there's a problem. As you go through this section you'll find that there are many questions that you are unable to answer. Even when answered, how sure are you of the accuracy? How many more questions can you think to ask? How much time and cost will it take to get accurate answers? Is it worth the investment to get accurate answers? Will the information or questions be obsolete by the time you've answered?

Therefore:

- **Compare analysis to practical experience.** When successful experience is in conflict with analysis it may be that you have not asked the relevant questions or have used incorrect data. It may also be that conditions have changed, and you'll be in trouble if you follow the path of experience.

- **Optimize results by testing experience against analysis, and analysis against experience.**

- **Analysis is no substitute for thinking.** Analysis is an aid to thinking. Don't mistake accuracy of the method for accuracy of the result. GIGO! (garbage in = garbage out.)

- **Test for reasonableness and consistency of results among several methods.**

- **There's no only way, or even best way, of deciding.** Use whatever fits your personality or is comfortable. But be careful. Discomfort with a procedure may indicate disagreement with your intuition, and intuition can be wrong.

- **Above all, the critical questions are human questions to be answered by people and not equations.** Why are you in business? What are your business objectives? What are your profit objectives? How do you want to treat people (employees, customers, competitors...)? These are matters that cannot be answered by a price-demand curve. Once you've answered these questions, however, analysis will help you achieve the results you're after.

2.2 Price

Price is the value or worth of something. It's the amount of one thing that is exchanged for another.

An exchange is a transaction between two parties, a buyer and a seller.

To properly understand the concept of a "price", and especially a particular price in a particular situation, we need to know about the buyer, the seller, the transaction, issues of worth, and value. Consider the following questions:

- **Who is the buyer?** Is it the ultimate (final) user; the individual that negotiates the transaction; the person who pays for the item, etc.

- **Who is the seller?** Is it the person who builds the item; the person who invented (thought of) the item; the individual that negotiates the transaction; the person who makes a profit or suffers a loss on the sale, etc.

- **Who decides on the worth or value?** Is it the buyer, or seller, or both? Which buyer and which seller?

- **Who sets the price?** The buyer, the seller, or both?

- **Is there more than one price**? For example: buyer asking price, seller offer price, final price, etc.

- **What is the buyer's objective(s) in setting a price?**

- **What is the seller's objective(s) in setting a price?**

- **What happens if buyer and seller don't agree on a price?**

- **Is there an "optimum" price for the seller?** How does, or should, the seller decide on what is "optimum"?

2.3 Value

Value is a perception or belief on the part of the buyer respecting the worth of something.

- **The buyer's needs, wants, financial condition, competitive offerings, seller's offering... all contribute to the perception of value.**

- **The buyer is not compelled to buy.** Therefore, the seller must provide value in order to sell.

- **Only sales provide income.** All other business transactions increase expenses. Without income there's no business; without sales there's no income; without value there's no sales.

The idea of value, and the word "perception" bothers some people. It seems nebulous, difficult to hold on to. That's true. But it gets very real when the price is not in line with the perception of value. You find out quickly, because there are no sales. Anybody can make a mistake here. And I do mean anybody, even a superbly managed organization like Hewlett Packard. Thus, the June 1994 issue of Electronic Business Buyer explains that H.P. PCs were not selling, and "Price was the culprit." What went wrong? It seems that the price was set on the basis of cost and not perceived value.

- **Successful pricing must meet the customer's perception of value.**

2.4 What does your customer value

What your customer values depends on the relationship between the customer, your business and your competitors.

- **Who is the customer?** Is the customer the end user or a reseller? Is the customer the person who wears the shoes, or a store that sells the shoes? Is the customer the person who lives in the room with the tile floor, the landlord who owns the apartment, the builder who built the house, the carpenter who changed the old flooring into the newer tile?

- **What business are you in?** Are you in the shoe business, or are you in the whatever people wear on their feet business? Do you include boots and sandals? Do you deal only with sport shoes? Perhaps only running shoes? Perhaps you deal with sport apparel of which sport shoes is one item? How about sport equipment of which clothing is only one item?

  Does the customer value being able to get all sporting needs in one location? Does the customer value having all possible shoes in one location?

- **Consider your competitors.** Who are your competitors? What do they offer, what are their prices, what's their business, who are their customers?

  If you're selling shoes do you also compete with boots? If you're selling floor tile do you also compete with carpets?

2.5 The competition

Customer perception of value and, therefore, your pricing behavior is affected by competition. You need to know and understand how your competitors behave and what they offer the customer. Here are some questions that you should be able to answer.

- **Who is the pricing leader, you or your competitor(s)?** If you change prices will they follow? If your competitor changes prices will you (or do you have to) follow?

- **Are you in a zero sum market?** Do more orders for you automatically mean less for them and vice versa, or are you together increasing the market size?

- **Who is the real competition?** Are you competing with a specific (i.e., individual) other company that's trying to sell to the same customers as you, or are you competing with a different (i.e., substitute) industry. For example, if you sell aluminum do you compete with another aluminum company, or against a plastic alternative?

- **Is the competitive environment a major, if not the primary, determinant in setting prices?** Would you set your prices differently if there were no competition? How much different?

- **Are you gaining or losing market share to your competitor(s)?** Whether you gain, lose or maintain position, is that what you want? Who's making it happen, you or your competitor(s)?

- **Who is the primary leader in establishing the customer's perception of value, you or the competition?** What does this do to your pricing strategy/flexibility?

2.6 Profit

Profit is what's left over after you've paid your expenses.

You may have a variety of business objectives, such as: to have a job, to be of service to the community, to perfect some invention or process, to be profitable, etc. Profit, and only profit, may not be your primary reason for engaging in business. However, no other objective will be achieved in the absence of profit. Therefore, you must consider profit when looking at pricing.

- **Do you have a profit objective(s)?**

  What is your profit objective, e.g., maximize return on sales, enough profit to finance Q% growth, achieve a set minimum ROI, etc.

- **In what way(s) is your product pricing affected by your profit objective(s)?**

  Consider both the type of objective and its level: i.e., % sales, internal rate of return, ROI... and level of objective such as 10% on sales compared to 15% on sales.

2.7 The ideal price

The ideal price will achieve your financial and other pricing objectives, and meet the customer's perception of value.

- **What you want to get for the price:** jobs, reputation, profit... you put into it time, reputation, cost, effort.

- **The customer is willing to pay for perceived value, involving:**

  - Personal want or need.

  - Product performance factors such as: speed, strength, size, quality...

  - Company performance factors such as: brand recognition, credit terms, distribution channels...

  - Competitor products and reputation.

  - Past history: yours and competitors.

  - Future expectation: do people expect a "better" product soon.

  - Price.

The ideal price:

YOUR OBJECTIVES ↔ PRICE ↔ CUSTOMER PERCEIVED VALUE

2.8 The price gap

You have a price gap when the actual price deviates from the ideal price either for you or the customer.

ACTUAL PRICE HIGH
YOUR OBJECTIVES ↔ DESIRED PRICE
ACTUAL PRICE LOW

ACTUAL PRICE HIGH
CUSTOMER PERCEIVED VALUE ↔ DESIRED PRICE
ACTUAL PRICE LOW

- **Why avoid a price gap?**

  A higher price than the buyer will accept will reduce, or eliminate sales. Can too low a price also be a problem? How about creating expectations for the future that you will not be able to meet?

A low price that doesn't meet your profit objectives could drive you out of business. Could too high a price be a problem? How about if it attracts many competitors (because they know how to do it for less) who will force you to reduce prices even lower than you need for survival?

By an interesting coincidence I just picked up the March 10, 1994 issue of *The Wall Street Journal*, which contains an analysis of the financial difficulties experienced by Euro Disney. The article states:

"Disney priced the park and the hotels more to meet revenue targets than to meet demand." Consequently, "The hotels have been just over half full on average, and guests haven't been staying as long or spending as much as expected on the fairly high-priced food and merchandise." ... "Many guests arrive early in the morning, rush to the park, come back late at night, then check out the next morning before heading back to the park. There was so much checking-in and checking-out that additional computer stations had to be installed."

"Disney executives have frantically lowered most prices in response, but high fixed costs and looming interest payments still are too great a burden..."

The above is an excellent example of an undesirable price gap. The price appears to have been set on the basis of costs and internal profit targets without full regard to customer perceived value. A higher price yields a lower demand. Hence hotels are only half full. Customers who are not satisfied with perceived value will do what they can to improve their position. Frantic check-in and checkout increased hotel service costs. Management cut prices to correct the gap. But a gap is still there because fixed costs will not be supported by current revenue. Hence, Euro Disney is in process of a major restructuring, etc., etc. Could all of this have been foreseen? I really don't know. Prediction after the fact is so much easier than before the fact. I do know that a little analysis beforehand can save much trouble later.

2.9 Price gap matrix

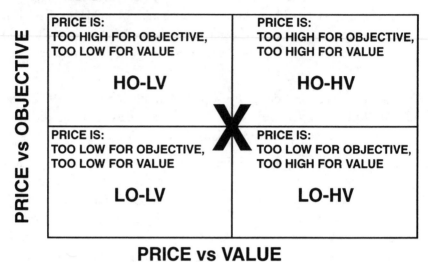

PRICE vs OBJECTIVE

PRICE IS: TOO HIGH FOR OBJECTIVE, TOO LOW FOR VALUE **HO-LV**	PRICE IS: TOO HIGH FOR OBJECTIVE, TOO HIGH FOR VALUE **HO-HV**
PRICE IS: TOO LOW FOR OBJECTIVE, TOO LOW FOR VALUE **LO-LV**	PRICE IS: TOO LOW FOR OBJECTIVE, TOO HIGH FOR VALUE **LO-HV**

PRICE vs VALUE

The X at the center represents the ideal price, all other positions introduce a price gap. It may take a great deal of effort to position the actual price on the matrix with a reasonable level of confidence. This is especially so with respect to customer perception of value. However, information gained from gap analysis can be well worth the effort.

2.10 Price gap matrix implications

- **HO-LV:** Great place to be if you know what to do with it.

- **LO-LV:** Fairly easy to fix with a price increase. But analyze first. Perhaps long term contracts work against a price change, or perhaps the price is right for product family comparative pricing.

- **HO-HV:** Theoretically easy to fix by a price reduction. But analyze first. There can be reasons why the price is right but the perceived value, or your financial objectives are wrong.

- **LO-HV:** You're in trouble. Reduce costs, improve perceived product value, or get out of this business.

2.11 Price gap analysis

You need to position the price within one of the four matrix quadrants before you can perform a price gap analysis. Don't bother with analysis if you aren't confident that you have the correct quadrant. In addition, you need to locate the price within the quadrant. There's virtually no practical difference in consequences, regardless of which quadrant you're in, if you're close to the ideal price in the center. The difference in results between quadrants can be very important, however, when the price is in an outside corner where the gap is large.

Analysis involves a consideration of possible consequences by answering a series of questions, such as:

- **Why are you where you are and how did you get there?**

- **Do you want to be where you are, and do you want or need to move?**

- **Where do you need or want to be?**

- **What do you need to do and what can you actually do to move to the desired location?**

Here's an example to illustrate the procedure:

- **Where are we?**

  You're priced at the upper left-hand corner of the matrix, where you exceed your objectives and customers perceive that they are getting a bargain. You might think that this is a great spot to be and it would be foolish to make any changes. Possibly that's so, but here's a scenario where change does make sense.

- **Possible consequences?**

  You'll soon have more orders than you can fill. People will be angry. Your distributors will come after you. You'll create a secondary (black) market at higher prices. You'll encourage theft from the factory. Your costs will increase to handle security and processing complaints about delivery. You'll get a bad reputation about service...

You decide to go for it by building a new factory to increase output. This means borrowing money. This can be risky. Perhaps the high order rate will not hold up as competitive or world conditions change. What will you do with the empty factory and how will you repay the loan?

You analyze why the demand is so high and decide that demand will not dry up. A new factory looks like a good idea after all, until you consider your competitors. They will not like what you are doing, and will fight back. The big guy will decide that you have to be stopped while you are still small. The big guy is 1000 times your size. You are a new company and this is your first and only product. The big guy could start selling a competing product below your cost, or spend more than all your sales for advertising, or whatever. Soon you could be out of business. Is a new factory still the way to go?

- **How did we get here?**

We developed a new process so our costs are half as much as the competition. Oops! Is the process patented, can we stop others from doing the same? How long a lead time do we have before others match our costs?

- **Do I want to move?**

Yes, where I am seems too dangerous. Given the market and competitor situation I consider the following alternatives.

First scenario: I'll change my profit objectives to gain even more percent profit than now by moving the price up to be closer to the 100% perceived value line. I'll continue to underprice my competitors to gain share, but not as much as before. This will improve my delivery situation and not upset my competitors as much. I'll build more output capacity with less borrowing by using my extra profits and improved cash flow. I'll also use some of the profit to develop new products so I'll not be a one product company.

Second scenario: I'll stay where I am and initiate a campaign to show customers that other products are overpriced. This will move the 100% value line towards my product on the left. Everyone that is now on the line will move into the "price is too high for perceived value" quadrant. My competition will not like it and they'll attack me. But I will form an alliance with a major financial power. My competition will see that they can not drive me out of business due to lack of money, so they'll not even try. Their best bet is to get out of this business, or perhaps pay me to license my new process. Either way I'll be number one in this business.

• **Conclusion**

There are, obviously, many versions to how this could develop. There are many ways to win. There are also many ways to lose, even in the pleasant situation of more profit than you know what to do with. An analysis, such as the above can avoid much trouble.

2.12 Price gap example

Here's a real-life example of a price gap situation that I was involved with:

The client is a division of a larger corporation. Total division orders/sales is $23.5 million (the analysis takes orders and sales as equal). The division decided that its product portfolio had a hole that should be quickly covered. Time was of the essence and there was not enough time to develop this product in-house. Instead, it was decided to purchase this product from another manufacturer for resale. The division marketing manager was asked to deliver $1.5 million in orders for the new product. This individual made a P-V analysis and concluded that the requested target was reasonable. Marketing expected to sell 430 units at $3,500 each. The purchase price plus other (variable) costs associated with handling and selling this product came to a total of $2,700. Hence, the product contributes $800 (800 / 3,500 = 23%) per unit to profit. The product was profitable at the desired sales level. Marketing signed up for a division target of $25 million, including $1.5 million from the new product.

But this isn't the end of the story. The division has various fixed operating overhead costs of nearly $1 million, and there is a significant corporate allocation of costs as well. This is all done on an absorption allocation basis as a percentage of forecasted orders. The total allocation comes to $7.5 million, or 30%. In addition, the division has an operating income before tax hurdle of 5%. Thus, accounting burdened the newly purchased product with a 35% additional cost. A $4,150 selling price was computed on that basis $(2,700 / (1 - 0.35) = 4,154)$.

VC = $2,700. Total sales target = $25M. Allocation = $7.5M. Allocation% = 7.5/25 = 30%. IBT hurdle = 5%. Total allocated price need = 30 + 5 = 35%. Product sales = $1.5M. Allocation$ = 0.3 * 1.5 = $450,000.

P (1000$)	3.0	3.5	3.9	4.15	4.5
Q	550	430	310	240	186
R (1000$)	1650	1505	1209	996	837
CPF	165	344	372	348	335
Profit after $ Allocation	-285	-106	-78	-102	-115

The above procedure involves a variation of break-even analysis. It will not work here because it assumes constant sales revenue regardless of price. The product was forecasted at $1.5 million of revenue at a $3,500 price. A P-V calculation yields revenue of only $1 million at a $4,150 price. Only two thirds (1 out of 1.5) of the allocation moneys will be absorbed by this product. The remainder will reduce the profit margin of other products.

Under these conditions we need to look for the price that will provide the highest level of contribution to margin using only variable costs ($2,700), regardless of the fixed cost level. This was found from P-V information at $3,900 and 310 units, for $1.2 million in sales. Thus, we have a contribution to fixed cost and profit of 310 (3,900 − 2,700) = $372,000. The fixed cost allocation that this product was originally intended to carry was 30% out of $1.5 million, or $450,000. This fixed cost really is fixed. It does not change regardless of price or sales. Hence, the best we can do is cover $372,000 of it. A higher price or lower price than that which optimizes contribution will yield less. This product cannot show a profit using full absorption accounting. Rather the best we can do is to show a loss of 450,000 − 372,000 = $78,000. Using a $4,150 price with 240 units sold (240 * 4,150 = 996,000), the contribution to profit is 240 (4,150 − 2,700) = 348,000, and the loss is 450 − 348 = $102,000. At the original plan involving a price of $3,500 and 430 units, the contribution is 430 (3,500 − 2,700) = 344,000, and the loss imputed to this product is 450 − 344 = $106,000.

This product is in the lower right-hand price-gap quadrant at a selling price of $3,900 per unit. The original price, established for market conditions based on customer perception of value was $3,500. The new price is too high for customer value. The price needed to obtain profit objectives is $4,150. The price is too low for business objectives. This is a most unpleasant place to be. But, $3,900 is the very best price in a bad situation. Any other price just makes things worse.

Now that we know what we are facing we can make a rational decision on what to do.

- The product does make a significant contribution to fixed costs. The corporate costs will not disappear if this product did not exist. Will corporate management be willing to forgive some of their allocation? Chances are that the answer is "no" once the sales target was accepted. This analysis should have been done in advance so that the allocation could be negotiated before the sales target was set.

- You can try to reduce the $2,700 cost by renegotiating the product purchase price. There's a good probability that you'll have to discontinue carrying this product given the current financial results. Your supplier may be willing to help you stay in business.

- Is there something that can be done in the market place? Can you enhance the value of this product so as to generate more sales or charge a higher price?

- Try for a combination of all three of the above.

- Perhaps you should start a crash program to build your own product as quickly as possible so your variable cost will be less.

- Re-examine the strategic importance of this product. Given what you now know, do you still want to keep it?

NOTE: Look at demand and break-even analysis in Chapter 3 if the above calculations seem mysterious.

Chapter 3
Pricing Procedures

3.1 Pricing sequence

The basic price analysis, or pricing sequence, was presented in the previous section. The essential elements of the sequence consist of the following.

- What is the value?

- What are the objectives?

- What is the profit?

- Is there a gap?

- Fix the gap.

A complete pricing strategy, however, may need to consider many of the following additional elements.

- Price-demand relationship.

- Market segments.

- Manufacturing capacity utilization.

- The experience curve.

- Relationship to other products.

- Impact on the future.

- New product pricing.

- Pricing in inflationary times.

- Incremental sales.

- Pricing for market stability.

- Defensive and offensive pricing.

- Bidding.

- Market growth or zero sum?

- Commodity or differentiated product pricing.

- Costing — absorbed or not?

3.2 The price demand curve

Maximum Demand Curve, Demand Schedule, Price Volume, P-V, Price Demand graph or curve are alternate names for a graph of the relationship between the price per unit (P) and the demand in quantity of units (Q), at that price.

- Total sales revenue (R) is the product, $R = P * Q$.

Here's an example of the basic relationship:

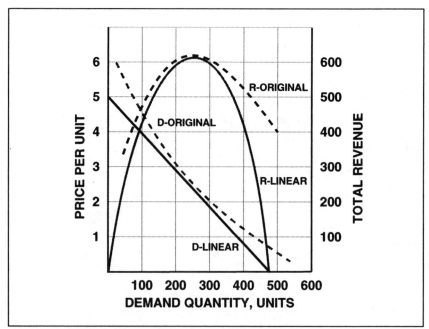

Figure 3.1. Price-Demand Graph — Basic Concepts.

You have somehow established an estimate for the demand of your product at particular prices. P is in monetary units, such as dollars or thousands of dollars or whatever. Q shows the quantity of units, and R is the total sales revenue in monetary units. See figure 3.1 for a graphical representation.

P	1	2	2.5	3	4	5	6
Q	460	300	250	200	130	90	50
R	460	600	625	600	520	450	300

At a price of $1 / unit you expect to sell 460 units and your total revenue is $460. At a price of $6 / unit you expect to sell only 50 units and your total revenue is 50 x 6, or $300. Neither the high volume at low price position, nor the low volume at high price position yields the best sales revenue. In this example, maximum revenue of $625 occurs at a price of $2.5 and volume of 250 units.

In many instances, especially where the P-V curvature is not great, it's convenient to approximate the price and demand relationship by a straight line. A straight line tangent to the curve at P = 2.5 also shows maximum revenue of 625. The straight line tangent intersects the zero volume position at $P_0 = 5$, twice the maximum revenue price of 2.5. Indeed, it can be shown that for a straight line demand relationship, the maximum revenue price is at one half the zero volume intercept. This, and other easy-to-use results, is a good reason for approximating the P-V relationship by a straight line.

3.3 Demand curve analysis

• Figure 3.1 shows a graph of the P-V example just discussed. We have four graphs. The original demand data is shown as D-original. The revenue is labeled R-original. A straight line approximation to the P-V data is labeled D-linear, and the revenue graph for that is shown as R-linear. Note that while the original and linear approximations deviate at the ends, results are pretty much the same in the center. In particular, note that both P-V representations yield the same maximum revenue results.

• Figure 3.2 shows two P-V lines of different slope. These illustrate different degrees of elasticity. You don't have much elasticity if a large

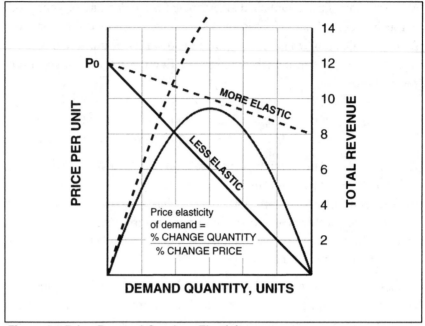

Figure 3.2 Price-Demand Graph — Elasticity

change in price gives a small change in units volume. Thus: % change in quantity / % change in price.

You don't have to be very accurate in setting your price in the inelastic case. Unit volume and sales revenue will not change much for a price change. Go for the higher price to keep your profits up when in doubt. But an incorrect price setting for an elastic situation can have a serious impact on sales and profits.

- Figure 3.3 shows a generic straight line version P-V relationship. The straight line simplification makes it easy to test for various assumptions, such as an approximation of total market potential.

This P-V straight line is based on connecting two points. First you estimate the price at which essentially no one will buy, (P_0). The second point is your estimate of the quantity of units (Q_0) that people could use if price were no problem. The area under the line, $P_0Q_0 / 2$, indicates total market potential. The potential market size, using this pro-

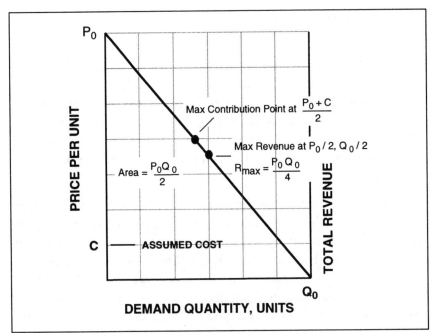

Figure 3.3 Price-Demand Graph — Total Market Potential.

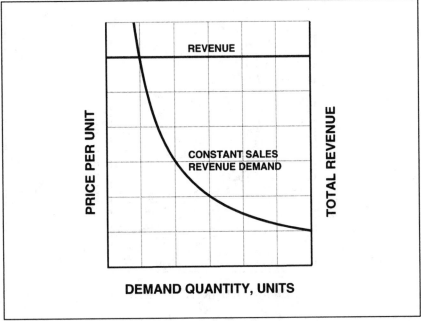

Figure 3.4 Price-Demand Graph — Constant Revenue.

cedure, comes to twice the maximum sales revenue which is at $P_0 Q_0 / 4$.

You should be suspicious if your estimate of total market sales (yours plus competitors) is well outside this calculation. Perhaps the "competing" products are not really competing for the same customers. Perhaps your estimate of competitor sales is wrong. Perhaps your demand curve estimate is wrong. Whatever the problem, you need to reconcile your estimate by computation with your estimate from other sources.

- A special case involves the constant revenue demand curve shown in figure 3.4. Here the greater the price the more the profit, because total sales revenue does not change. But quantity of units does change. The question is, what happens to the additional unit volume if you increase the price? Do fewer people use the item, or do they go to the competition? Before you set a very high price you need to consider how long you will be in business if the competition controls 99% of the market.

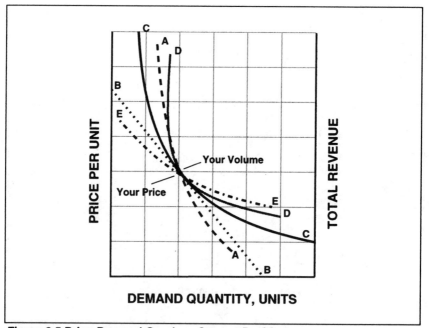

Figure 3.5 Price-Demand Graph — Current Position.

- There's only one point that you know exactly on the P-V graph, the price and volume for your own product. An infinite number of different shapes can be drawn through this point as illustrated in figure 3.5.

Assuming you are not after a major change in price and strategy, then you only need to know the P-V shape, mostly the slope really, in the vicinity of your current position. The constant revenue case can be a good comparison reference. The more elastic curve "E" improves in revenue at slightly lower prices and greatly increased units, while less elastic curve "A" shows maximum revenue at a higher price.

- Usually the P-V relationship is part of a family involving different grades, performance levels or alternate product types that are related to each other. This is illustrated graphically by figure 3.6.

Examples:

- Alternate performance levels — Luxury automobiles compared to get-me-to-work at a reasonable price cars.

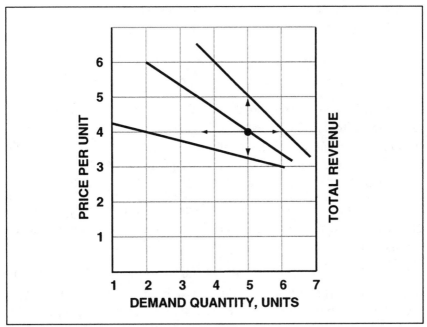

Figure 3.6 Price-Demand Graph — Family.

- The same item aimed at a different customer group — The same food in a wholesale, get-it-in-bulk and package yourself, place vs. a specialty food shop.

- Substitute alternates — A plastic table vs. a solid wood table.

Knowing which items you really compete with and which curve you are on can be important. Knowing which curves are around you can help guide your pricing and "perceived value" positioning. Knowing what is around you will help your position versus competitors.

Consider the family of three P-V lines in figure 3.6. Your volume is 5, but it could be 6 if you could jump to the higher curve. Or, you could move your price from 4 to 5 without loss of units volume if you could move to the higher curve. Suppose your competitor does something that drives your product to a different competitive mix? Suddenly your price needs to move from 4 to 3.2 if you are to maintain your volume, otherwise the volume will drop from 5 to 2.

3.4 Demand curve with cost

Consider the price and volume relationship shown in figure 3.1. We have the following information.

P	2.0	2.5	3.0	3.5	3.7	4.0	4.5	5.0	5.5
Q	300	225	200	170	160	135	106	90	70
R = PQ	600	625	600	595	592	540	477	450	385

The revenue numbers show total sales. But there's a manufacturing cost associated with these. We need to deduct the manufacturing cost in order to find how much these sales contribute to profit. Thus, for a per unit cost of $C = 2$, the contribution to profit (CT) is found at:

CT = (P-C) Q	0	113	200	255	272	270	265	270	245

For a cost of $C = 3$, the maximum contribution to profit drops to under 200 at a price near $P = 5$. The higher the cost, the lower the maximum attainable contribution no matter what we do to the price.

- Notice that the price at maximum contribution is less than the maximum revenue price plus cost. For a straight line P-V the difference is $C / 2$ as shown in figure 3.3. The maximum revenue price is 2.5 in our example and the maximum contribution price is 3.7. The straight line value would be 2.5 + 2 / 2 = 3.5.

- For a given P-V relationship it's not possible to fully recover the impact of higher costs no matter what you do to the price. Furthermore, the higher the cost the higher the price for maximum contribution and the new maximum is smaller than the previous maximum.

- You move toward the edge of the demand curve as you increase the price in an attempt to recover higher costs. This can be dangerous because:

You never have accurate demand curve information, and the accuracy is usually worse at the edges.

Even if the information is accurate, you're dealing with low unit quantities at the high price end. Therefore, you can no longer rely on statistical averages to smooth out individual customer differences. An adverse change to just a few customers can have a big impact.

Your competition can target the few customers that you still have, on a one-on-one basis.

- **Conclusion:** Cost control is a critical factor in pricing strategy.

3.5 Profit

Profit is what is left over after you pay the expenses (costs).

Costs are of many kinds:

Fixed	Variable
Product related	Not related to the product
Long term	Short term
Engineering	Marketing
Manufacturing	Administrative

- You have fully absorbed costing when all costs are somehow attached, or allocated, to a product.

- You have direct costing when fixed costs, which accumulate even if you don't build or sell anything for a while, are separated from the variable costs associated with the production and sale of products.

- Standard costing uses historical information to establish what the cost should be, and the actual value is compared by way of variances.

- The variable cost works very nicely with the demand graph. Subtracting the cost from the price leaves per unit profit (actually contribution to profit, or just contribution, because there are additional costs).

The maximum profit contribution price is greater than the maximum revenue price. For a straight line demand curve the increase is $C/2$. This is a good approximation in any case, because the graph can be approximated by a straight line for small changes.

- It's not possible to fully recover a cost increase through a price increase.

- A cost reduction is a powerful way to improve profit.

Therefore:

- Any cost increase to build or improve the product must increase the value to the customer so as to improve the P-V demand position. Otherwise, profits will suffer.

3.6 Cost analysis examples

How you treat costs can have a major impact on your perception of profit, and hence your price needs. Indeed, it's not at all unusual for individual products, or a whole product division, to be discontinued after a change in cost accounting methods. I personally have a bias against strict absorption accounting by means of allocations, and favor a more pragmatic approach. That doesn't mean that you should do it my way. Whatever you do, however, you need to know what you are doing, why you are doing it this way, and what the consequences might be. Analysis and consequences is illustrated by the examples that follow.

Absorption accounting example:

You sell five products, each with sales revenue of 20 ($20, or $20,000 or 20 million, it makes no difference). The total sales revenue for your business is 100. The total fixed expense for the business is 45, and variable product related costs are as follows:

product	var. cost %	variable cost	:	fixed cost	total cost
A	@ 70%	(20) (0.7) = 14	:	+9	= 23
B	@ 60%	(20) (0.6) = 12	:	+9	= 21
C	@ 50%	(20) (0.5) = 10	:	+9	= 19
D	@ 30%	(20) (0.3) = 6	:	+9	= 15
E	@ 20%	(20) (0.2) = 4	:	+9	= 13
Total variable cost =		**46**	:	**total cost**	**= 91**

The fixed business cost is 45, the total variable cost is 46, and total business cost is 91. Total sales revenue is 100 and profit remaining after all costs is 9% of sales.

You wish to analyze profit on a by-product basis. You, therefore need to absorb all fixed costs, which you will allocate on an equal percent of sales basis. Each of the 5 products has equal sales of 20 and the allocation yields 45 / 5 = 9 cost points per product. The absorbed cost per product is shown in the total cost column.

The total cost for product A is 23, while sales for the product is only 20. It appears that we are losing money on this product. Product B also looks like a loser. So we decide to improve our profit by discontinuing these two products. Eliminating A and B, however, does not change the fixed costs. So we now allocate 15 cost points to each of the remaining three products. Products C and D now appear to be losing money, so we discontinue these as well. Product E now has to carry the full fixed cost burden, and it clearly can't do it. Therefore, we close up shop and go out of business.

A 9% profit on sales may be less than we would like, but it's a long way from losing money. Our analysis procedure clearly didn't enhance our decision making process.

Direct costing example:

You look at the revenue and profit results for products A, B, C, D, and E (these are not the same products as in the previous example). Sales for each is 20. Cost for each is 19, 10, 8, 7, and 6 respectively. Profit for each is 1, 10, 12, 13, and 14 for a total profit of 50%.

A 50% profit is fabulous. We have money to burn. No we really don't have excess money. We have a 50% contribution to profit, but the profit itself is less because of fixed costs.

Suppose the fixed cost for the business is 40. This yields a 10% profit. Dropping the least profitable item reduces sales revenue to 80, and profit with respect to sales improves to $9 / 80 = 11.25\%$.

3.7 Additional cost analysis

The fact that fixed costs don't change with product volume is true only for a period of time, but not forever. If you drop volume to zero, by going out of business for example, then the fixed cost eventually goes to zero too. Fixed cost is in some fashion connected to the product, though the connection may not be simple.

Why do fixed costs have to be allocated on an equal percentage of sales basis to all products? Different products do impact fixed costs in different ways. A product that involves an elaborate waste treatment plant has a different fixed cost component than one whose manufacture doesn't create toxic waste, for example. Allocating the fixed cost on other than a simple % of sales basis can lead to totally different business decisions. You can only do this, however, when you have information on the relationship of products and fixed cost.

The result for the previous example on absorption costing would look quite different if we had better information on the connection between fixed cost and products. Suppose product B were responsible for 15 points of fixed cost out of the total of 45. Furthermore, this is cost that can be eliminated over time if product B were gone. Then, eliminating product B will reduce the total fixed cost to 30. Total sales goes from 100 to 80 and the variable cost of the remaining four products (A, C, D, E) remains at 34. The total cost is 30 + 34 = 64, the absolute profit is 80 – 64 = 16, and percentage profit increases from 9% to 20%.

The above doesn't really prove that we should eliminate product B, but only that we should consider it. It may take much time and cost to phase out this product and all associated fixed costs. Possibly the loss of product B will adversely impact people's jobs that we don't want to eliminate. Perhaps product B is what attracts customers to the other products.

3.8 Break-even analysis

Break-even analysis combines the effects of fixed and variable costs.

A break-even analysis answers the question: given a certain fixed cost and a known variable cost per unit, what is the units volume quantity that we have to sell to break even.

You break even when enough units are sold for the revenue to cover all expenses, fixed and variable. This is illustrated in figure 3.7.

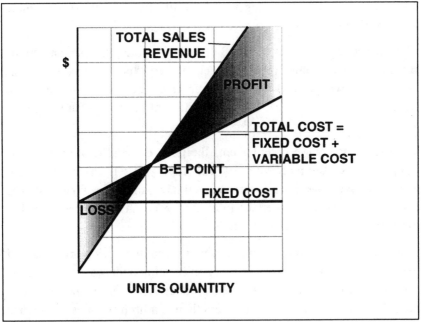

Figure 3.7 Break-Even Analysis.

Consider the following example. For a fixed cost of 100, a variable cost of 10 per unit and a selling price of 20 per unit, the break-even point is at 10 units.

```
sales =            20 * 10 =      200
variable cost =    10 * 10 =      100
fixed cost =                      100
Costs (100+100) =    sales of 200
```

A break-even analysis is not a single method cure for pricing analysis complications. For one thing, it is not possible to vary unit volume at will at a constant price (remember the demand curve). However, it is an important addition to help you make an intelligent decision. This technique is particularly useful for incremental sales analysis, and capacity utilization decisions.

3.9 The experience curve

Like sports or a musical instrument, or anything else, the more you do something the better, more efficiently, you usually do it. The experience curve is a graph showing the improvement in efficiency, by way of lower costs, the more of something you do (build more units, service more items, sell more, etc.).

The experience curve (see figure 3.8) looks like the price-demand curve. But the number of units relates to accumulated experience as more units are built, or whatever else you do over time. It costs less to build 100 units after building 100,000 than to build 100 units after building only 1,000.

The experience curve complements the price-demand relationship. The lower the price the more you sell. The more you sell, the more experience you have. The more experience you have, the lower your cost. The lower your cost, the lower the price that you can afford to offer. The lower the price, the more you sell.

This, perpetual motion seeming, chain of reasoning does work. Much of the enormous gains in cost per function in semiconductor electronics is a result of experience curve based productivity improvements. But it doesn't work well for everything, and there's a limit to gains even when

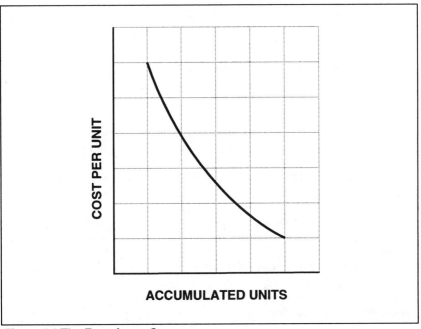

Figure 3.8 The Experience Curve.

it does work. You don't want to emulate the fellow who was losing money on every sale but promised to get it back on volume.

- You may want to initially lose money and deliberately price below cost, if:

  - You expect significant cost gains from volume experience.

  - Cost/price is a key market position driver.

  - The market is price sensitive. A lower cost will quickly generate volume to give you cost reducing experience.

  - The competition will soon have a competing product. They might do it to you, if you don't do it to them first.

  - The competition is too far behind in time to catch up on the experience curve. Potentially they will give up and let you keep the whole market.

- This is a dangerous move. You can lose a great deal if you are wrong. But, you gain much if you are right.

3.10 Incremental sales pricing

When and why should you do it?

- You have excess capacity. You can deliver more product without an increase in fixed cost, and possibly even lower variable cost due to more experience.

- You need work for people. People will lose jobs if there's no work for them, or you will have increased costs due to idle direct labor.

- You are in financial difficulties. A little more volume to cover fixed costs will help pay the bills.

- You are convinced that a lower price will generate more volume.

Then:

You can offer a lower price on a temporary basis to generate additional, incremental, sales you would not otherwise have.

Implications and cautions.

- You can not be controlled by an absorption accounting system where all fixed costs are equally allocated to all sales.

- You need to have good cost information: by product, by fixed vs. variable costs, etc.

- The market/customers will permit a temporarily lower price. The new price will not become permanent.

- Your competition will let you do it. They will not match your price and cancel your volume increase. Worse yet, you will not start a price war spiral where everybody loses.

3.11 Pricing for the future

Why worry about the future?

- Most people would like to be in business in the future as well as in the present.

- Even if your price is perfectly correct today it may still be wrong in the future because of competition or other market/customer changes.

Inflation may make your current price too low to meet profit objectives, or volume experience may make your price too high, etc.

- You need to consider what the critical future related issues are for your business and/or product. These need to be considered in product pricing. The analysis and result depend on the particular issues. Consider inflation, for example.

A relatively high rate of inflation, say 1%/month, will cut your profits, all else remaining unchanged. One reason is because you pay for your material and labor months before you are paid for what you sell. The unit money you pay is worth more than the unit money you're paid.

Your customers have the same problem as you do, and wish to compensate by reducing costs. Your customers will resist a higher price, and actually push for a lower price.

What can you do other than blindly increase the price?

- Can you manage by taking a lower margin till the inflation subsides? Perhaps, but only if you have good profits to start with. At 1%/month you lose 12.7% for the year. How long can you do that? How do you know how long the inflation will last? Making no changes can be a recipe for disaster. On the contrary. Changes should be made quickly, and aimed at meeting needs well into the future (at least six months) so you will not need to make very frequent adjustments.

- Analyze the customer and market price sensitivity for your business or product.

Is the market segment particularly sensitive to value involving such things as performance or service? If the customer base needs or wants value enhancing attributes (e.g., luxury market, or safety issues), then you can concentrate at being best in those areas and charge the customer accordingly. You might actually gain share against competitors who try to cut cost/price by reducing value.

If your customers resist higher prices, then your most effective way to maintain profit margin is to cut costs. Reducing cost is a more effective way to improve profits than raising prices in any event. Once you have reduced costs you will be in a better competitive position even after inflation subsides.

- What if you have to go with a price increase even though your customers object? Try to provide additional value that pays the user for the increase. For example, your operating costs require a 4% price increase or you will be out of business. But, for an additional 1% cost you can provide a feature that saves your customer enough operating time to be worth 4%. You may choose to increase the price by 5% and provide the feature so your customer loses only 1%.

  What if you cannot add additional features, and you need a higher price? Consider unbundling. Instead of selling a complete system, perhaps the customer can choose the best combination of price and features as needed to provide useful value.

- How do you know how much additional margin you need for the future? You decided on a six-month calculation because that happens to be the time from when you pay your costs to when you are paid for your goods. Could you possibly cut the time from six months to three months so your receivables turn at four times per year instead of only twice? Perhaps your customers will be happy to pay faster in return for a lower price increase?

- What if you face the opposite of a luxury market? Can your customer manage with a few less features? Is there something that contributes just a little bit to the customer but costs a great deal to make? Can you remove this feature and hold the price steady, or even reduce the price?

- Remember that whatever you do, you must provide value to your customer. You will be out of business if your customer can not stay in business. But different people value different things. Who really is the customer? Look at market segments for an answer.

3.12 Market segmentation

Effective market segmentation is the key to analysis and successful pricing.

What business are you in? Who are your customers? What do they need, want, and value that you provide? Who are your competitors (companies and products)?

A different answer to these questions will provide a different perspective on your business. "We're in the motion picture distribution business" would provide for the sale and rental of video tapes. But, "we provide motion pictures to be shown in theaters" does not. Our business and pricing behavior will be different for the two because the theater segment of motion picture viewing, or distribution, has different characteristics, needs, and value parameters than the video tape rental segment.

- **A market or customer segment involves a group of buyers (or potential buyers) with similar needs and value concepts.**

The perceived value, and appropriate price, will differ for the same product from segment to segment. For example. Automobile users that commute to work in heavy, stop-and-go, traffic have different ideas about automobiles than large family users that take driving vacations.

Choice of which segment(s) to compete in will affect your pricing decision. And a misunderstanding about which segment you really compete in will usually adversely affect your business results.

- **A market segment involves a subset of customers who value substantially similar product or service parameters, and whose interests and/or needs and/or values differ sufficiently from others to be differentiated and treated differently.**

A segment should be broad enough to be worth addressing, but sufficiently homogenous to be treated as an entity. Too wide a segment tends towards low value for a large number of participants. Too narrow a segment provides high value, but for very few people. Either way, your sales revenue suffers. A well thought out segment involves useful value for an attractive number of people. Choice of proper segments in terms of characteristics and grouping size is an art that comes with much, and continuous practice, and a deep and subtle understanding of your business and customers.

- **Choose the segments for your business, or overall market, on the basis of externals: customer interests or needs, competitor behavior or offerings, the world economic or political situation, etc.**

- **Choose which segments to compete in or emphasize on the basis of internals: what are your strengths, where can you make a differ-**

ence, what are your interests, where can you win, etc. Just because there's a segment out there doesn't mean that you have to aim for it.

3.13 What's the right price

Your objectives ↔ **Price** ↔ **Customer perceived value**
Financial objectives   Product related value
Other objectives   Service related value

- The intent is that the price be a bridge connecting your objectives and customer needs/desires so that you can sell, the customer can buy, the seller makes a profit, and the user gets value.

- Unfortunately, there's a third party in this relationship — competitor(s).

Your competitor interferes with you and adds to your costs because the competitor offers value to the customer.

3.14 The strategic triangle

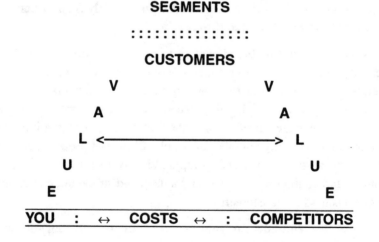

You and your competitors cause each other additional costs.

You and your competitors provide value to the customer(s).

The value you provide and the value your competitor(s) provide are compared by the customer(s). Different customer/market segments will react differently to what you and your competitors offer. You're paid a price by a customer when what you offer is judged acceptable, desirable, and more valuable than what your competitor offers.

Your analysis needs to consider the customer (segments), competitors, and yourself. This is not a linear progression with a clear start and finish. The process is highly iterative. Thus, for example, you need to analyze your customer segments, but your choice of segments to serve is based on knowing who you are and what you want. You need to analyze yourself, but choice of strengths and weaknesses for detailed scrutiny depends on what your customers value. This procedure is more of an art than a science. You can learn about procedures from a book, such as this one, but you will only learn to do this well by actually doing it.

3.15 The customer

- The usual first step is to consider what business you are in (or want to be in). What products or services do you offer (or intend to offer). What's your basic business objective, and what's your superordinate objective. For example:

  We deal with pharmaceuticals and, in addition to an acceptable return to shareholders, we need profits so as to research new drugs. However, our superordinate goal is to alleviate chronic pain, and in particular find a cure for arthritis.

- Define the market and customers for your business. This means that you describe market segments. The impact on distribution is quite different, for instance, depending on whether your arthritis drug is aimed at hospitals, doctors, the pharmacy owner, a pharmacist, an arthritis patient.

- Use whatever technique is comfortable for you, such as demand curve comparisons or a price-value chart (see 3.19 and 3.20), to analyze the segments in terms of "value" contributing components and, if possible, assign a numeric "price" value to each component.

- Assign/develop value ratings for your products and competing products. How do these compare? Do you have a gap?

3.16 Competitors

You need to identify, describe and understand your competitors. Consider whatever is appropriate to your business situation.

This includes:

- Identify your competitors with respect to specific customer/market segments.

- Which competitor's products compete with which of your products.

- Identify and describe competitor company/division/products strengths, weaknesses and general characteristics such as:

  - How important to them are these products or markets?

  - What commitment have they shown to this business in the past?

  - How much commitment can one expect from them in the future?

  - How do they appear to have segmented the market?

  - On what basis do they appear to compete? For example, price, performance, brand loyalty, etc.?

  - What is their sales volume?

  - Etc.

- What is the perceived value of their products?

- How do their prices and perceived value compare to our prices and perceived value?

- Is there anybody else who might become a competitor in the future?

- Is there anybody now who is currently a hidden competitor by means of substitute products?

- How does the competitor view us (i.e., is the concentration on the customer or is the aim to hurt us)?

- Etc.

3.17 Our business

- Who and what are we? Are we a small division of a very large company or are we the primary business of the company?

- What are our pricing objectives for the business, for the company, for the product, for the market (segment)?

  - Maximize profits. How? % sales, ROI, cash flow...

  - We want stable profits that will not drop below a specified minimum.

  - Sales growth. Quantify rate.

  - A stable business (price) environment.

  - We want to have a high quality image.

  - We want to serve the community, society, mankind. Define "serve".

  - We want to create new jobs. What kind?

  - We want to price so as to protect existing jobs.

  - We want to provide value for shareholders via dividends or the stock price.

- How well are we achieving our objectives?

- What is the perceived value of our product(s) (per segment)?

- Do we have a gap between price and perceived value?

- Do we have a gap between results and objectives (especially financial objectives)?

- What do we need or want to achieve in the future?

- Etc.

3.18 Market environment analysis

You have previously looked at segments. Here we want to consider the overall market environment. Consider:

- Overall market growth now and in the future. (We might switch to a different segment if the total market is growing, but our segment is not.)

- Market stability and predictability. (The oil business became unstable in the 1970s due to war in producer areas.)

- Level of competitor rivalry. (Do competitors cooperate to hold prices stable and grow the market, or do they try to put each other out of business.)

- Consider the economy involving inflation, ease of borrowing, jobless rate...

- How secure is the supplier chain involving cost, stability, and reliability of suppliers.

- What is the state of technology? Might a substitute product be on the horizon?

Now connect the above to your segments to see if all is in order. Are product, customer and market relationships changing so that current conventional wisdom on segments no longer applies? For example, the specialty stores that sold our product are disappearing. Now it's mostly large department stores that sell our product. Our business is now doing well. But will it do well in the future if we don't re-segment the market to consider that large department stores use a different "value" mix than small specialty stores?

3.19 Assigning customer value

For a particular product with respect to a particular market segment, who determines the value? The user, the buyer, someone else? Consider children's shoes. The child (user) and parent (buyer) jointly determine perception of value. One contributes $X\%$, the other contributes $Y\%$ and together we have $X + Y = 100\%$. You need to analyze both and combine in proportion to X & Y weights.

List all the important factors that contribute to the customer's perception of value. To find out what these are, ask the customers, look at complaint and suggestion letters, ask the sales people, etc.

Assign a numeric rating of importance to each factor. There are a variety of methods for doing this. Here are two common procedures:

- Assign 20 points for most important, 19 points for next important, down to lowest points for least important. This method requires rank ordering of all the factors. No two factors can have equal importance.

- Here's an alternate procedure. Assign 20 points to the most important factor. Then assign any value, up to 20, for other factors. Two factors can have equal importance.

- For your product, and each competing product, assign 10 to the best available in each factor. Assign proportionally less than 10 to each lesser capability.

- Compute customer perceived value as the product multiple of customer importance ranking and product/company contribution.

Example:

Customer factors		My Product		Competing products A		B	
			Value		Value		Value
Return policy	18	10	180	10	180	8	144
Available colors	10	9	90	5	50	10	100
Hard to break	20	7	140	9	180	10	200
Easy to assemble	18	9	162	10	180	9	162
Works fast	12	10	120	10	120	10	120
Small size	20	10	200	8	160	9	180
Not noisy	10	5	50	7	70	10	100
Looks nice	14	9	126	7	98	10	140
Easy credit	10	10	100	10	100	10	100
800 number	10	10	100	0	0	10	100
Total value			1,268		1,138		1,346

Competitor product B is judged to have best customer perceived value.

A numeric calculation is just one way to do it. There are other ways to estimate perceived relative value among products. For example, you can ask a selected focus group of customers to assign ratings.

An estimate is the best you can ever have for customer perceived value. There's no absolute number here as for price. Furthermore, it's a constantly changing value because competitor behavior and customer needs and interests are not stable.

Make an educated guess based on your experience if you have nothing better. A guess followed by analysis, in turn followed by market results and more analysis will eventually lead to a reasonable estimate of customer perceived value.

Having established a perceived value index you can now make a graphical comparison of the price-value relationship between competing products as shown in figure 3.9.

3.20 The price-value comparison graph

Price versus value comparison information, such as provided in figure 3.9, is useful in setting an appropriate price. Consider the following hypothetical situation.

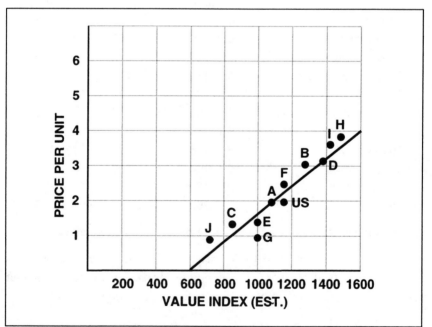

Figure 3.9 Price-Value Comparison.

Our product, marked, "US" in figure 3.9, falls well below the best straight line approximation of the price-value relationship for its market segment. Apparently customers expect a higher price than we are charging. Therefore, we would expect our unit volume to be higher than normal, and more than for product F of equal value but higher price. Is it? Our best estimate of competitor product F shows that we don't sell more than F. We are actually selling fewer units than F.

But wait, F is a competing product, how do I know the volume? Perhaps it was published in an annual report or a market study. Maybe I did a customer survey. Maybe I checked serial numbers over a period of time. Using some such means, we get an estimate of sales volume for product F.

Based on best available information, it appears that sales volume for our product doesn't fit the profile expected from figure 3.9. What's wrong?

- Perhaps sales volume for product F is not as high as we think.

- Perhaps we don't really understand the customer segments and F is in a totally different segment from us.

- Perhaps the customer values something where F is better that we didn't consider.

- Perhaps all the analysis is correct except that the customer isn't aware of all the qualities of our product. Remember that the value has to be perceived by the customer.

- Perhaps the end user whose preferences we analyzed is not the purchase decision maker.

Whatever the answer, we need to understand this inconsistency. A better understanding will lead to action aimed at improving our business results, such as new advertising so people will know how desirable our product really is, or move to a new segmentation scheme, etc.

3.21 The price gap revisited

We discussed the price gap matrix in section 2.9. Here's how to connect the matrix and the price-value graph.

- A price-value comparison graph, or a ratio computation of prices vs. computed value points, or analysis of customer survey information, or some other type of price and value information will show you how well your price fits the customer perceived value. This information is not accurate. Therefore, test the result for consistency via price-demand analysis, sales volume compared to other products, etc. You will never be certain that your conclusions are correct, but you need to be satisfied that your conclusions could be correct.

- You do have accurate information on how well your product meets internal objectives.

- Construct a price gap matrix using the information from above.

The price can be just right or too high or too low with respect to your profit objectives, and/or with respect to perceived customer value. The four quadrants of the matrix are as follows:

The price is too...

High vs. Objectives (profit)	**High vs. Objective (profit)**
Low vs. Value Room to move price up or down. Can have big impact on market structure or strategy.	**High vs. Value** Move price down or need to move value up.
Low vs. Objective(profit)	**Low vs. Objective (profit)**
Low vs. Value Potentially adjustable by increase in price. But it can be difficult, because price increase can cause customer resentment.	**High vs. Value** Trouble. Hard to fix. May need to readjust product or market choice. May have to exit or take strategic loss.

Whatever you do, make sure to analyze strategic business implications such as impact on other products, or competitor response possibilities. Note that doing nothing is a perfectly legitimate option.

See also 2.12 where the P-V relationship is used as an indicator of customer perceived value.

3.22 Sources of profit

You have only three direct sources of primary profit: more price, more unit volume, less cost.

Only lower cost is a sure winner of profit. More price or more volume may actually cut profit because these interact with each other. Therefore, never neglect attention to cost.

The direct sources of profit are affected by numerous indirect sources. For example, higher customer value can lead to more price or more volume, and lowering bad debts cuts costs.

Profit may mean different things under different circumstances. Return on investment or a payback-period hurdle rate may cause a "profitable" product to look less than desirable, and vice versa. If your big worry is meeting the payroll next week, then cash flow may be more important than return on sales.

3.23 Other product (lines)

Attention to maximizing results for one product without considering the impact on other products, or other product lines, can "win the battle, but lose the war" for you. Here are some examples:

- This product appears to provide very little, if any profit, so you phase it out. But the calculation is based on full absorption of allocated fixed costs. Loss of this contribution to fixed costs can destroy the apparent profitability of your other products (see example in 3.6).

- This product appears to provide very little, if any, profit so you increase the price. You expect that unit volume will go down by 50%, but you are willing to accept that. However, most people that buy this product also buy a very high margin product. Most people don't want to go to two places, they buy the products together. By reducing sales on your low margin product you will also reduce sales volume for your high margin product, and total profit will decline.

- You have 50% of the unit volume and your competitor has the other 50%. You're convinced that a 15 unit reduction in price will give you most of the competitor's sales. You're also convinced that the competitor will not change price. Your current contribution margin is 50 units and it will drop to 35 after the price change. A demand curve analysis shows that unit volume will increase from 100% to 175%. Hence, contribution to profit will change from $50 * 100 = 5,000$ to $35 * 175 = 6,125$. A gain of 1,125.

However, this product sells for only 30% more than your next lower performing product, of which you sell 5 times as many units at an equal per unit margin. After the price reduction on your better product, 40% of the lower priced product users switch to the better product at an almost equal price. Thus, your profit contribution was originally $100 * 50 + 500 * 50 = 30,000$. Now you have $[175 + (0.4 * 500)] * 35 = 13,125$, and $(0.6 * 500) * 50 = 15,000$. The total profit has dropped from 30,000 to 28,125.

- Some feature of your product is difficult and costly to make. You'll reduce costs by eliminating this feature. You expect no change in volume because you'll reduce the price in accordance with the perceived value of this feature. You expect improved profits because the reduction in price is less than the savings in costs. But the change in performance moves your product to a different price-demand curve (see figure 3.6). You lose volume and profits.

- Your main competitor derives 50% of revenue and profit from one product. Your competing product provides 10% of your total revenue and profit. You have left each other alone because you don't compete much. Now this competitor has announced intentions to compete in your main markets. How will you respond?

You can do many things to defend your main products and markets, such as reduce cost, improve performance, or reduce price on your mainline products where you will soon have strong competition. But there are many possibilities and you don't know which of these your competitor will emphasize. What if you concentrate all your efforts to cut cost, improve value, and reduce prices to minimal margin on the product you now compete in?

You will gain sales from your competitor who will have to spend resources to defend his main market. These are resources not available to attack your main market. If you get into a price war, it will affect only 10% of your revenue but 50% for your competitor. Your competitor may have to abandon plans to move into your market due to a lack of resources.

Cross subsidizing products, as above, can also work at cross subsidizing geographies. Perhaps you should aim at a lower profit margin in the geography where your main competitor gets most of the revenue in order to prevent this competitor from using local profits from attacking you in other places. Note, however, that there are laws against "dumping" (selling below cost), so be careful when using a cross subsidization strategy.

3.24 Impact on the future

Current prices must take into account the objectives for the future of the business. Otherwise there might not be a future. Here are some examples:

• Consider the experience curve. If you develop a totally new product, or new ways to provide existing products, then (due to lack of competition) it may be possible to charge a higher price than your profit target requires. This isn't necessarily bad for the future. You might change your strategic profit target and invest the extra earnings for future growth. Alternatively, you could reduce prices significantly, gain volume, cut costs as you gain experience and assure future dominance of this market. Your choice involves many strategic considerations. The key is to recognize that setting a price is equivalent to establishing a strategy. The price is the way the strategic choice is announced and implemented.

• If you decide to enter a new business area involving significant new investment, and if you are used to absorption accounting, then: the current profit target could drive you to relinquish some of your current markets due to high prices. Remember that the price must be in reasonable balance with customer value. Your decision to enter a new business doesn't contribute to current customer value.

- To avoid the difficulties of frequent price behavior changes in the future, your initial price should take into account future cost of labor, materials, inflation, etc.

- Imagine that your superordinate business goal is to provide employment opportunities in your community. This drives your desire to make the business grow. Growth needs funding either from borrowing or profits. Assuming no dividend payout and no borrowing (to simplify matters), the sustainable growth in sales is approximately the ratio:

% profit / [% (assets / sales) – % profit] [2]

If you have a high asset utilization business with an asset level at 90% of sales, it takes 18% return on sales to fund a 25% growth rate. Thus: 18 / (90 – 18) = 0.25.

Your objective is to provide jobs for people. You are not much interested in profit. Yet, you must price to gain 18% on sales in order to get the job growth that you want. Maybe you should change your business pricing strategy to emphasize asset utilization. If you could increase your asset turns to a ratio of 2:1, then for a 50% asset base you need only a 10% profit level to fund 25% growth. Thus: 10 / (50 – 10) = 0.25.

3.25 In inflationary times

No business procedure is instantaneous. It takes time to develop products or services, to install machinery for production, to train people to sell or service the product, etc. The expense precedes the income. Profit must take into account the cost of the delay involving cost of borrowing to pay expenses before there's income, and erosion in worth of income due to inflation. Various financial measures are used to take into account the present value of past investment and the present value of future income.

- The payback period is a simple calculation of how long it will take to recoup the initial investment. A $30,000 investment has a three year payback if we earn $10,000 per year once sales begin.

---

[2] See: Higgins — *Analysis for financial management.* ISBN 0-256-03004-9.

- Net present value computes the present value of past or future income, taking into account the reduced worth of income as we move into the future. Assuming a 10%/year discount rate (because that's the cost of borrowing, or that's the forecast for inflation, or some other basis), then the present value of $1 a year ago is $1.10, and the net present value (NPV) of $1 a year hence is 1 / 1.1 = $0.909. If we earn $10,000 per year for three years, then the NPV is: one year @ $9091, two years @ $8,264, three years @ $7,513. The total is $25,228, and not $30,000.

If the $30,000 investment in the payback calculation was invested at $10,000 now and $10,000 each in previous years, then the present cost is: 10,000 + 11,000 + 12,100 = $33,100. The fourth year of earnings has a net present value of 7,513 / 1.1 = $6,830. Total four year earnings is worth $32,058, just under the present value of the $33,100 investment. Therefore, the payback period, including inflation, is over four years and not three years.

Pricing with inflation needs to take account of the changing value of money over time (see 3.11).

3.26 Pricing a new product

You will seldom go wrong if you follow a why, when, what, and how routine.

- **Why are you introducing this new product?** Is it to replace an older product at a better value or cost/price; is it to enter a new market; do you want to complement an existing product (line); are you looking to match the competition; etc.

- **When are you doing the pricing?** Is it an estimate for an R&D go vs. no-go decision, or are you ready to announce and sell the product, etc.

- **What are the competitive, customer and internal factors that impact choice of price?**

Consider strategic and financial internal factors associated with this product. For example. We are entering a new market and other products will follow if this one is successful. Then we need to consider impact on current products and markets. For instance, maybe the new product should be announced under a new brand name to decouple it from current products. State financial pricing objectives including type and numeric level: return on sales (how much?), contribution to fixed costs (how much?), payback period (how long?), etc.

Consider the relationship between the price and the competition. How will they react and how will we respond? Have we chosen the best price with respect to competing products?

Consider pricing with respect to customers and market segments and associated segments for related products (both yours and competing). Look at price-demand, growth rates, relative value factors, price change history, etc.

Consider the overall environment involving such things as the global economy, trends in technology, supply/availability of raw materials, inflation and capital availability levels, user cyclical behavior such as fashions, etc.

- **How, and at what level, should we set the price to best meet our objectives in the current and projected customer, competitor, and internal company environment?**

Use whatever procedures best fit the situation. Is there a price gap? Do a gap analysis. Look at alternatives. Do you want to shift to a different segment? Do you still want to announce this product? Consider alternatives such as: a low price with learning curve strategy, or a high price prestige positioning strategy, or a high initial price and meet competitor price as needed later. What can go wrong with whatever you decide to do? Prepare a contingency action plan.

3.27 Incremental sales

Pricing for incremental sales means that this price is an exception, and not the rule. See 3.10 for a discussion on why and when to do this. To succeed, you need good information respecting: fixed and variable costs, impact of price on volume, your capacity level and ability to output more product, freedom to price differently in the future, competitor price response.

Use a combination of price-demand and break even analysis to determine the financial impact of various prices. Margins will likely be very low. Therefore, the penalty for a miscalculation can be severe. You could end up shipping money with every sale. Do a max, min, most-likely analysis to estimate how much trouble you could get into.

3.28 Pricing for market behavior

Here are some example scenarios.

- You're looking for market stability in a large and growing market, and your primary interest is to keep the market growing and customers happy with the current situation. Then you should not introduce any significant price or value innovations that will change the market structure. You move into the unknown when you cause a change. Are you sure you'll be better off when the dust settles?

- You have most of the market. Things are pleasant till a new competitor comes along. This is an old and stable market. There's no room for growth. Anything the new competitor gains is a loss for you (see 3.30, zero-sum). You must defend immediately and vigorously if you don't want to lose your long-term position. This will involve lower profit, at least for a while. Consider selective pricing on a cross subsidy basis, a general price reduction, re-segmenting the market, product value enhancements, increased customer support, more sales channels or effort, promotion changes, etc.

- You are the new competitor looking to gain share from the current market leader. Don't go directly head-to-head against an entrenched and superior competitor. Try for a target segment that isn't critical, or threatening, to the superior competitor. Don't present a fixed target. Move about so the competitor can't focus on you, and arrange for lots of bank credit to withstand a long war of attrition.

The above is not your only choice. If you believe that the competitor is vulnerable because you have good cash flow credit and a high manufacturing cost advantage, then you could aim directly at the main source of competitor revenue. Your competitor will not be able to afford a major price reduction.

Your strategic choice depends very much on what you expect your competitor to do. As much as you need to focus on delivering value to the user and profits to yourself, you need to focus even more on the expected behavior from the competition.

3.29 Bidding

The bidding process can go through several stages such as technical performance acceptance, agreement on terms and conditions, etc. Eventually it usually comes down to lowest price wins. You need to consider five items in setting a bid price.

- What's the lowest price at which you're willing to accept this business? This isn't necessarily the actual bid price, but the absolutely lowest price you will accept. Anything lower and you'll be satisfied to let your competitor win. Incremental pricing is an important factor in this decision.

- Your estimate of the competitor's bid price (high, low, likely). What should your bid price be for an acceptable probability of winning (e.g., 95%). You might make a graph of bid price vs. % probability of winning.

- How does this bid relate to your overall strategy?. Perhaps you choose to bid high knowing that you'll probably lose. But you know that a bigger bid opportunity is coming up and your current bid will help you win the next one at a higher than normal price.

- What will you do if you lose, what are your contingencies? Do you want to change position on the other items, especially the lowest affordable price, in view of what will happen if you don't win this bid.

- Is there a gap between an acceptably high probability of winning and the lowest price? Is there anything you can do about it, such as change the product or service to reduce costs. If the gap is in the other direction, then how greedy do you want to be by bidding a higher price? Consider your gain in profit versus a lower probability of winning.

3.30 Market growth or zero-sum

Here's a nice place to be. The market is clamoring for what you offer. Neither you nor your competitors can supply enough product. Consider the following in setting a price:

- Why and for how long will this go on? Is there enormous market growth with no end in sight, or is this a temporary shortage?

- Are you in this market for the long term? Do you want to be in this market just one more year or ten more years?

- What position are you looking to achieve long term vis-a-vis your competitors, e.g., equal, bigger, smaller?

- How strong is brand or product loyalty? Will current customers stay with the same brand/product in the future?

- How badly do you need the profits from higher prices you can charge at this time?

- What does a higher price "umbrella" do to attract new competitors?

There's no panic to buy, but the market is growing nicely and is projected to continue into the future.

- Are you getting your needed, desired, "fair" share of growth?

- Is a calm and stable market contributing to growth?

- Are stable prices contributing to good, or at least acceptable, margins?

- How will your competitor(s) react to aggressive pricing?

- Is there room (via re-segmentation perhaps) to offer more value at a higher price, and thereby improve margins?

- How elastic is the market, will the market grow much faster at a lower price?

The market is stagnant, or even shrinking. Your business will shrink if you don't take share from competitors.

- What's your capacity utilization? Do you gain at lower priced incremental sales?

- Is your competition vulnerable in some area? Market segment, product performance, customer value perception....

- What are your strengths and weaknesses compared to the competition, customer values, etc?

- How badly does your business (survival) depend on this product or market?

- Can market growth be revived via new product types, features, prices, services...?

- Can you cut costs to improve your position?

- How badly does your competitor depend on this market? How hard will your competitor fight to retain or gain share?

- Can you reposition to a different segment scheme?

- Should you get out of this business?

3.31 Commodity

- Are you satisfied to compete primarily on price?

- Do you actually prefer to compete on price?

- Do you have lowest costs? Do you expect that this will continue?

- Are you well down the experience curve and your volume is greater than for the competition?

- Is price a very significant factor in the purchase decision?

- Will you continue to invest in procedures and technology to keep your costs lowest (not just low, but lower than others)?

- Are prices low but stable at a profitable (for you) level?

Then:

You may wish to compete on a commodity basis.

Can you successfully compete as a commodity, where price is the controlling factor, if someone else has the lowest cost and best experience curve position? Not likely. Competing on price requires relentless attention to costs. However, even a "lowest" cost position may not be enough to keep you out of trouble. Your competitor may not realize that your costs are lower, and be willing to "temporarily" lose money to gain share. Possibly an inexperienced new competitor will misjudge experience curve cost gains, etc.

Luckily, you don't have to be a commodity. There's no such thing as a pure commodity. It may take some work, but if you look hard enough you'll find differences between you and the competition. Is there absolutely nothing in the customer value set where you can be different (hopefully better)? What about service? What about distribution channels? What about training? What about bundling or unbundling with other products? What about re-segmentation? What about selling to the performance-focused end user, rather than the price-focused purchasing agent?

Chapter 4
Introduction To
Strategic Behavior

4.1 Why behavior

This section is titled strategic behavior, and not strategic thinking, or strategic planning, or strategic something else. The reason is that thinking, planning, making decisions, gathering information, etc. are important elements in developing strategic skill and establishing business strategy. But there will not be any results unless you actually do something. All the thinking, planning, and strategizing is just a way towards effective, efficient, and successful behavior. Only by doing, on an ongoing basis, will the thinking and planning yield results. The ultimate intent is to achieve the desired result which represents success in the business.

Strategic behavior results from a combination of planning, thinking and action. Thus:

Planning — A semi-formalized process for devising future objectives and procedures.

Thinking — To exercise the powers of reason, judgement, inference, and reflection. To form a mental image.

Act — Do. A state of real existence rather than possibility.

Strategic — That which is of great importance within an integrated whole, to a planned effect.

Behavior — The response of an individual or group to its environment. Winning behavior results from planning + thinking + action. Such behavior is strategic.

The aim of strategic behavior is to achieve results which are representative of business success. This includes establishing the type and level of result desired, the planning of procedures and stratagems to achieve the results, and executing the actions that achieve the result. A strategic plan is not a business result. It's the content of words describing a strategy. People employed, sales growth achieved, % profit delivered — these are business results. Jobs lost, loss of customers, looming bankruptcy are also business results. Successful strategic behavior aims at achieving desirable business results and avoiding, or reducing, undesirable business results.

Strategic behavior is a vast topic. Strategy, planning, finance, people management, business operations, marketing, manufacturing, the psychology of behavior, and much, much more have a bearing on strategic behavior. Frankly, I don't feel qualified to try for a full treatment on this vast array of topics. Certainly, it would take much more than this modest book, let alone one section of the book, to do so. The aim of this section, as indicated in the title, is to merely provide an "introduction", rather than an exhaustive treatment. I have been guided by the following five points in preparing this material.

- I believe that what happens at the interfaces between business functions determines the difference between failure and survival, and mere survival and success. Strategic behavior is a critical element at the interaction between functional organizations such as sales and manufacturing. We, therefore, need to introduce this topic in any discussion on business success.

- All managers and supervisors, and indeed all employees, need to focus on strategic behavior.

- Strategic behavior, in this book, is taken as a supporting element to pricing strategy. This section emphasizes those elements of strategic behavior that are important to pricing issues and ignores other elements of the topic. This means that planning in general, and strategic planning in particular, is covered to a fair degree, while organizational structures and human resource management is pretty much ignored.

- While I cannot provide a full discussion on strategic behavior, I believe it useful for the reader to get a feel for the full range of the topic, and particularly how I view it. I have, therefore, included a number of illustrative stories and statements of personal opinion. These don't claim to represent any absolute level of truth. Valid exception can be taken to everything I say. Therefore, take care not to follow any of this advice blindly. Use what makes sense to you and fits your needs, and ignore the rest.

- No doubt much of what is presented in this section, and the book as a whole, is applicable to all sorts of businesses whether manufacturing, service, or merchandising. The reader should keep in mind, though, that my experience and writing is based on a manufacturing business perspective.

4.2 You are in charge

Congratulations! You're now part owner and a corporate officer of Wonderful Widgets Inc., due to a legacy from Uncle Joe. What a surprise. You only met him once, 23 years ago. Being an owner and manager at WWI means that you have:

Management obligations — The right and responsibility to formulate and implement decisions and policies.

Authority — The legal right to give instructions, make job assignments, hire and fire people.

Power — The right or opportunity to make things happen, get people to do various things or behave in certain ways by virtue of your influence or authority to give orders.

These are serious responsibilities that will affect your life, the lives of others and the fortunes of WWI. What you do and how you do it will be determined by what you want for yourself, for others, and for WWI. But wanting is not the same as getting. Other managers may oppose your ideas. There may be government regulations against what you want to do. Employees might not cooperate. The competition might get in the way. In short, it's not sufficient to decide on what you want to do. You need to plan on how to do it. You also need to decide on how soon you want to see results and how much of your life (job, income, reputation), and WWI fortunes you want to risk.

You can approach these issues in many ways. One way is to establish a primary objective, or superordinate goal. Do you want to be the builder of the best and most wonderful widgets in the world, or do you want to be the person that brings a widget into every home? If the latter, then perhaps you should change the name from "wonderful" WI to "universal" WI. Along with the change in name comes a change in strategy. You'll need more factories to build more widgets. But it takes money to build factories. You'll have to convince your banker to lend you the money. Etc.

The above involves deciding what, when, why, and how to do, the plans to achieve the objectives and execution of the plans. All of this together constitutes strategic behavior. This also applies if you are not a corporate officer or company owner. You still have responsibility, authority and power at whatever your job is. People disagree with you and refuse to cooperate. You still have to consider what you want, plan how to get it done, and then carry out your plan. The sphere of influence and operations is different, but strategic behavior is still strategic behavior. The scope of the game is different, but the rules are the same.

4.3 Plans

A plan can be defined as a scheme, design, or method proposing a mode of action aimed at attaining some purpose. A plan is also the physical document where the scheme, action, and purpose is described. Certainly, having a physical embodiment of the plan is important, for communication if no other reason. But the essential value of the plan is in the content, rather than physical form. And even the ordinary content in its linear representation, as in a book read starting at page one, does not attain maximum worth. Rather it's the totality of the plan, the full image that you have in mind, with myriad interconnections and digressions, that yields the fullest return on the planning effort. This is why, experiencing the planning process is frequently itself the best reward for doing it. Whenever possible, all who need to understand and carry out a plan should be involved in developing the plan.

Plans can be trivial or critical, take a moment's reflection, or months of difficult work to develop. We plan all the time. We plan the menu for dinner, a vacation trip, purchase of a new car, choice of education or career, how to find a new job, what choice of treatment to pursue when a serious illness strikes. Clearly some of these items are more important to us than others, and the penalty for failure much more serious. Generally, long-term plans of a global nature, such as what education and school to choose based on an analysis and decision respecting a lifelong career, are considered strategic. Short-term plans involving local action, such as setting the time to go shopping for dinner groceries, are usually considered tactical. Another view is that tactics is a subset of, and driven by, strategy. A means for carrying out the strategy. Such a distinction is useful when dealing with planning. My primary interest in this discussion, however, is not in strategic planning, but in strategic behavior. Behavior involves not only the plan but also the execution of the plan. Tactics, especially action-oriented tactics in support of strategy, is a critical factor in strategic behavior. Furthermore, not all short-term or local matters are tactical in nature. What if the dinner, in the above example, is for your prospective in-laws? How the dinner works out could possibly have as much impact on your future as your choice of school. For purposes of this discussion, therefore, I'll take it that all plans, whatever the global level or strategy versus tactics designation, contribute to strategic behavior.

4.4 Analysis of a failure

There's nothing that better demonstrates the need for strategic behavior than to look at a failed attempt. The name of the organization has been disguised to protect the guilty. Otherwise, the information presented is true.

A number of years ago a corporation, which I will call Grow Inc., decided to significantly increase market share of one of its business areas. This business involved a certain type of electronic product, which I will call Testers. Grow had only 1% of the Tester market share, but this business accounted for about 10% of total Grow's business. Hewlett Packard (H.P.) was the market leader in Testers with over 60% share. Consolidated financial data shows that the business segment into which Grow placed Testers (about 30% of Grow total) was quite profitable. There's every indication that Tester sales contributed to that profitability.

Grow went out of the Tester business four years after embarking on a strategy to significantly increase share. The remainder of the business segment survived one year longer and was also phased out. A few years later I was given, for analysis, a copy of the Tester strategic business plan that started all of this. What follows are excerpts from my report.

"The Grow plan for Testers is an extensive document of 87 pages. The plan contains all of the important elements such as — competitive and market analysis, market and product segmentation, discussion of corporate objectives, setting of strategies to achieve the objectives, etc."

"The plan spends quite a bit of space on projecting future technological trends and forecasting the result on Testers. They rightly predicted 'replacement of analog with digital storage media, increasing use of digital logic to control functions, on-board microprocessing, computer compatibility...' and various other trends."

"Using future H.P. product projections based on the above technology forecast, plus product segmentation by frequency, the authors of the plan conclude that 'there are no price or performance gaps of any significance in the H.P. product line.' Therefore, they conclude that the appropriate 'strategy is to compete head-on with H.P., offering products equal or better than theirs.'"

"The corporate goal was for a 20% market share in four years compared to about 1% when they started. This represents more than a doubling of business every year if we ignore the projected 8% CAGR for the market. Furthermore, the number two competitor after H.P. is projected to grow from 13% share to 20% share. A little computation shows that H.P. would have to lose one third of its market position during these four years. This miracle was to be achieved via a massive new product development program."

"The result of this program is that H.P. ended a bit stronger than before, while Grow went out of the Tester business. What went wrong?"

"The obvious place to blame is engineering. They never came through with the necessary products. But then, how could they when management never gave them the necessary resources defined in the plan. Furthermore, the management goal of growing from 1% share to 20% share — while also holding before tax profits at 13% — is ridiculous to start with. From a strategic point of view however, I consider the planning at fault."

"1. The financial analysis is inadequate in several areas. For instance, a cash flow analysis would show that Grow could not muster the projected new product development resources."

"2. There are no contingency plans. The plan details the necessary engineering resources but, given the difficult nature of the strategy, a fallback position should have been provided."

"3. The segmentation scheme is too simple. The one dimensional scheme gives the impression that H.P. has everything covered without 'gaps', thus, to grow it was necessary to go `head-on'. To win 'head-on' it's necessary to have greater staying power than H.P. — clearly beyond Grow's resources. A head-on strategy creates a win-lose situation, and as the Grow plan points out, 'H.P. has a tremendous head start... H.P. would have to essentially stand still'."

"Only a differentiation strategy, which sets up a win-win possibility, can succeed against a superior and determined competitor. The key to differentiation is market/product segmentation and business definition. These are the factors that stand between possible success and almost certain failure. It's easy to forget this as we concentrate on more immediately pressing issues."

It's no use belaboring the situation by covering a few more pages with excerpts from my analysis report. Obviously Grow was better off before they embarked on the ambitious plan to significantly increase their Tester business. Much of the blame in my report points at the strategy or strategic plan. But it was not really a bad plan when viewed in isolation. It's only when viewed in the ability and willingness to execute in light of internal resources and competitor strength, that the plan looks unworkable. In other words, it's the total "behavior" that is at issue and not the plan itself. There's nothing new here. Others have said it before me:

"Many of the problems of... corporations are related to execution rather than strategy... The company must pace its strategy according to its resources rather than going all out to achieve too much too soon. It must guard against overreaching itself."
Kenichi Ohmae. *The Mind Of The Strategist*

"Many companies fail to achieve their objectives, not because their strategies have been poorly formulated but because they have been poorly executed. Whereas formulating strategy is 'thinking a good game,' executing strategy is 'playing a good game.' Success in business depends on both."
Robert A. Stringer. *Strategy Traps*

"Competitive strategy involves positioning a business to maximize the value of the capabilities that distinguish it from its competitors. It follows that a central aspect of strategy formulation is perceptive competitor analysis... Who should we pick a fight with in the industry, and with what sequence of moves? What is the meaning of that competitor's strategic move and how seriously should we take it?"
Michael Porter. *Competitive Strategy*

"Only a clear definition of the mission and purpose of the business makes possible clear and realistic business objectives. It's the foundation for priorities, strategies, plans, and work assignments... Strategy determines what the key activities in a business are. And strategy requires knowing 'what our business is and what it should be'."
Peter Drucker. *Management*

A clear definition of the mission and purpose of the business, combined with realistic business objectives that are within the scope of available resources and in line with competitor strengths and likely reaction make for an achievable strategy. Whether the results are achieved or not depends on the skill and dedication with which the organization pursues the objectives. But at least the possibility of success is there. An intent 'to beat the unbeatable foe' makes a good song, but it doesn't make good strategy.

4.5 Variety of plans

Marketing plan
Corporate plan
Strategic plan
Business plan
Strategic business plan
Sales plan
Financial plan
Operating plan
Communication and promotion plan
Organization structure and people plan
Business portfolio plan
Etc., etc.

There's no end to the names or variety of possible plans. Neither this chapter, nor this book, provides a full treatment on plans or planning. You likely already have an established procedure involving type and structure of plans anyway. And there's no obvious one best way to do it. Reasonable people will differ as to the planning process and plan structure and content. All will agree, though, that the plan or planning is not the ultimate objective. Planning or writing plans for planning's sake is a waste of time, and can create a climate of false security. Only a plan that leads to behavior aimed at business success provides value added.

Different plans can be structured in the form of a hierarchy. Various plans being subordinate to, and supporting other plans. The operating, or manufacturing plan along with the marketing plan could be elements of the strategic business plan. Sales and promotion plans are sometimes part of the marketing plan. A financial plan could be the result of, and subordinate to the business plan. Sometimes, though, the financial plan is the driving force and the business plan structured to achieve the desired results. Elements of a plan, or a subordinate plan, may be called tactical while the overarching plan is termed strategic. I have my ideas on how it should be, but I don't consider it important for the topic of this book. My key premise is that price is a primary "glue" element that holds everything together and whatever plan or planning procedures you use it contributes towards strategic behavior.

4.6 Predicting the future

Planning is for future events which have not yet happened, unlike the past which cannot be changed. Events that have not yet happened are taken as unknown, while events that already happened are taken to be fixed and known. Predicting the future has a feel of magic about it, such as gazing into a crystal ball. It almost seems silly to try. So let's change the word to forecast, which has a more comfortable feel for me. Many things about the future can be known with essentially absolute certainty. I have no doubt, for example, that the sun will rise tomorrow just as it did yesterday. Furthermore, just because the past has happened, and cannot be changed, doesn't mean that we really know it. A forecast of the future has a likelihood, or expectation probability attached to it. So also has much of the past, which is not truly known to us, even though it has already happened. Past and future are much more alike than it would seem on the surface. It's mostly in the need to discover the "truth", and the procedures whereby this discovery is made, that past and future deviate.

We don't need to know much about the past for business reasons. Usually, a summary of final results is sufficient. But the future is different. We do need to forecast expectations in order to choose a course of behavior. One way to forecast the future is to extend, or project the past. Here we do need accurate and detailed information about the past. But not for its own sake, but for the sake of the future. To know the past usually involves research to discover facts and records of facts. A well run business will maintain a careful record about the present so it will be available for extension into the future when the present becomes the past. In this respect, knowledge of the past yields to effort, care, and record keeping. Not so the future. Projection of the past into the future is fairly easy via mathematical curve fitting techniques, or regression analysis techniques. Procedures are discussed in the literature and computer software programs are available. But there's always the possibility of a totally new event — A new scientific discovery that obsoletes your product, an earthquake that destroys a critical resource, or whatever. Here the idea is not so much to predict and project as to postulate and prepare. Such preparation involves contingency planning. Every plan, whether marketing, business, operations, or whatever, needs a contingencies section. This section provides behavior possibilities should an unlikely, but possible, emergency or opportunity develop.

4.7 Building a plan

An individual skilled in the analytic approach, involving analysis and the case method taught in business schools, might start with the raw facts and reason to a conclusion. Others will start with an intended result and build a case to support it. Some might say that starting with an intended result is like putting the cart before the horse. I don't see it that way. There's nothing wrong with starting with an intended result. Indeed, long-range strategic planning must start with objectives as there is no hard data available to show an unambiguous future. But you must be careful not to cheat as you try to justify the intended result. Some individuals have a powerful intuitive sense that seems unerringly to lead to the right objectives. Nevertheless, the hard work of analysis must not be bypassed, because intuition can be wrong. The key to success in this approach is intellectual honesty. It's very difficult to admit to others, and especially oneself, that your initial intent was flawed. Some people will go to great lengths to justify an initial idea that simply will not work. Just remember that what cannot work will not work. It's better to admit this early among your friends before the market does it to you later before your competitors.

Setting objectives is an iterative process. Analysis of preliminary objectives leads to permanent ones. The analysis needs to consider internal factors involving company resources and culture, and outside factors involving customers, competitors, and the world at large. Numerous books and articles are available with suggestions on how best to do this. Objectives should, as much as possible, be clear, concise, and quantifiable. Vague statements of philosophy should be avoided. Except in a few instances, such as human resource or staffing plans, objectives need to include a fair level of financial results.

Objectives identify what is to be accomplished. The plan will indicate how this will be accomplished. There's a need for detail and rigor so people can know what to do and we have good confidence that success can, and hopefully will, be attained. Again, the process is iterative. The objectives lead to tentative ideas, options, and alternatives. Analysis based on internal and external factors leads to a preliminary plan. A reality and consistency check of the preliminary plan leads to a final plan.

Functional plans, short term plans, tactical plans, and budgets form the supporting structure for the long range plan. These can be incorporated into the main plan itself, or as is usual, prepared as separate entities. The procedure is the same as before. There are objectives, plans, analysis, etc.

In addition to the many types of plans discussed starting in 4.5, there are also sometimes master plans involving portfolio, life cycle, technology, or other focus areas. There would be no time to do anything but prepare plans if every possible plan were prepared with full analysis and rigor. This we must not do. Preparing plans is a process and not a business result. The plan is not even second in line after results. The plan leads to behavior and the behavior leads to results. There's no result without implementation and execution of the plan. Some military strategists say that a bad plan, executed well, is better than a good plan, executed poorly. I would not go that far. A bad plan should not be executed at all. But I would certainly agree that a reasonable plan, executed well, is much better than an excellent plan, executed poorly. Therefore, don't do more than you need to. Sometimes, just a few words jotted down on one sheet of paper is a perfectly adequate plan. The emphasis must always be on doing.

4.8 Fit plan to need

Sometimes a full menu plan is not the solution to a need. Like the saying goes — it's hard to concentrate on draining the swamp where the alligators swim, when an alligator is chewing on your leg. First you must get rid of the alligator that's about to kill you. Then you can drain the swamp to get rid of all other alligators.

A while back a client asked me to comment on business expansion ideas and to develop a full business plan. My response was a surprise. I was opposed to the idea that I prepare a business plan. First, I noted serious problems which could kill the business before a business plan could be implemented. Secondly, the purpose of a plan is not just to have one. The plan must lead to effective action. And it's well established that implementation is seriously weakened when those who need to carry out the plan are not involved in the planning process. Therefore, a consultant should never be the sole author of a business plan. What I did, instead, was to provide a list of questions and suggestions. I prefer a question and answer format to a straight narrative. An outsider, such as consultant or whoever, can ask questions based on experience and objectivity that a fully involved individual will frequently not ask. By answering the questions, the fully involved individual will know what to do and the task will be carried out more effectively compared to instructions from outside.

In this instance, the issues involved a high growth potential business. I was asked for advice on how to choose sales agents in the Pacific Rim area where high sales growth was possible and also to suggest a total business plan. My concern was that the business not win the battle but lose the war. There was a need for balance between growth and: cash availability (from inside or outside), profit return for original investors, output capacity capability involving special machinery and skilled labor, maintenance of operating control, output quality, etc. Only after these matters were clarified could a business plan be set in place. Here's a short version of the questions:

Growth issues:

- What's the current output rate; compare to full capacity utilization?
- What's output capability for people, machinery, facilities?
- What's manufacturing asset turn rate?
- What's build cycle time?
- What's delivery time customers expect? Can you build to order?
- Do you now build to order or build to plan?

- Consider current cash flow and extrapolate self-funded growth rate?

- How much and for how long can you add additional cash for growth? What growth rate does this represent?

- Consider turmoil vs control as you grow — 30% easy, 50% possible, above 100% risky.

- You'll need to add people as you grow, and these will not be as productive initially as your current, experienced, employees. The work involves skill. Hence labor cost is not low. I estimate that you need a minimum of $75,000 in sales per employee to maintain desired profit margins. Consider the implications of growth vs profit in this light.

Outside marketing agent issues:

- Why do you want to bring in these people?

  - More current sales and profit.

  - Build up market share for future profit.

- Do you need a quick payback or can you subsidize long term?

- How much home office management time can you commit?

- Do you need local technical expertise regarding training, installation, repair, etc., or will you support from home office?

- Do you need local language literature? Who will supply?

- Who will control local prices and other sales conditions?

- Are there export control issues or other sales restrictions?

- What is available margin vs manufacturing cost for choosing a distributor discount?

- Should this be a sales agent or stocking distributor?

- Who handles currency conversions, international bank credit, and other collection issues?

- How much time, effort, and cost do you want to spend to investigate prospective agents?

- Have you considered a very short-term arrangement? You can learn by doing and dissolve partnership if you chose wrong partner.

- You need careful control regarding agent binding you to something you don't want.

- Which of your product (types) will you export? Remember the long logistics trail. Emergencies are costly. What chances are you willing to take respecting long-term liability to gain current sales?

Plans:

The usual procedure is to first develop a strategic plan and let the operating, manufacturing, marketing and other plans follow on a support basis. Here, however, I felt that the growth target issues should drive the process. Hence I recommended that operations, staffing, production, finances and other matters associated with growth and expansion internationally be well understood before a full-blown strategic plan be undertaken. The planning model involves iteration and consistency between functional group plans, operational plans, and objectives. The full range of plans, shown below, represents draining the swamp. I recommended that we not rush, and take at least a year to do this, because doing this well was more important than doing this quickly. But addressing the expansion issues could not wait as that alligator was killing us right now.

Functional plans	Operational plans	Analysis and iteration
Strategy	Strategy	Consistency, fit,
Marketing	Tactics	and gap analysis
Manufacturing	————	vs each other and
Sales	Operations	objectives.
Staffing	Logistics	

4.9 Plan content and structure

There are probably as many suggested strategic plan arrangements as there are books or articles on the subject. Preparing a plan, any plan, is as much an art as a science, and there are many ways to do it. Most plans have the same content, though. The differences are in structure, emphasis, and depth of detail. A useful way to choose the structure is to consider for whom the plan is intended. There are four possible plan users:

- The first user group consists of the people who prepare and write the plan. Ideally, this will be the managers and/or group supervisors who will need to carry it out. Sometimes a strategy staff consultant may also be involved. But this individual should only have an advisory function. The plan should be written with the help of this person, but not for this person. The hard work in preparing a plan is not in putting words down on paper. That is a matter of mere mechanics. What to say and how to say it is much more important and difficult. Having gone through the research and discussion involved in preparing the plan document, the authors are not likely to forget or misunderstand the essential content or intent. Many of the supporting details can be left out by referencing supporting documents, meeting minutes, or personal notes. The authors simply need a good outline and summary as a guide to future action.

- A larger group than the first involves the many people who will carry out the plan details. A terse summary will not suffice here. There are two primary objectives when addressing this group. Individuals need to be sold on the plan. These people need to believe that the plan is doable and that the intended result is worth the effort. Resource availability information and management commitment and support are important buy-in factors. Building support and enthusiasm for the plan is important, but it's not sufficient. The second point is to provide sufficient supporting details to permit the plan to be carried out. Frequently these details are not part of the main plan but in supporting functional plans, such as marketing and manufacturing, or tactical documents involving business operations. Usually it takes small group briefings to explain the plan and answer questions before implementation is attempted. I cannot overemphasize the importance of getting things right at this stage. The plan will be an utter failure, no matter how brilliantly conceived, if it's not properly carried out.

- Corporate management is the third focus of the plan. These are very busy people. A well structured overview, or summary is a must here. Likewise, expected business results, especially financial, will be of special interest. But don't just stick to happy promises. Things can go wrong. Make sure that the risks are understood. A well reasoned contingency discussion will go a long way towards neutralizing concerns about risk. In addition to explaining what you want to achieve, you must detail the resources it will take to do it. Be very specific on what it will take to do the job, and be sure to ask for the resources you need. Remember that the plan will fail unless you are provided the needed resources.

- Your final concern involves outside investors. Most strategic plans don't go outside the involved business. Corporate management, in effect, act as the outside investor who is looking for a return. Sometimes, though, a strategic plan is written specifically for presentation to an outside investor group. This may be a banker, venture money group or for private stock placement. Here the issues are very focused on cost, risk, and return on investment. Here you need to show that you know what you're doing; that you have a good understanding of the risks and probability of success is good in spite of the risks; and the return on investment meets acceptance criteria assuming you succeed. You need to do your homework and find out what criteria of acceptance your investor follows. This will usually be some combination of financial ratios such as internal rate of return on capital, cash flow, or percent income on sales, along with other factors such as market share or sales volume. Make sure to do your homework here, and be sure that you present a complete, clear, and consistent picture.

- The last item to consider is how long and elaborate the written plan should be. Here, more is not always better. The plan needs to be complete according to the needs of the group involved. But complete is not the same as long and elaborate. It's much more difficult and time consuming to write a concise yet complete plan, than to write a long and rambling plan. The long plan may appear complete because it contains every conceivable item. But it's also time consuming to read and difficult to follow. Anything that takes much too long to explain is probably something that you don't well understand yourself. Therefore, take the time to get things down to the essential essence. The people who need to read and implement the plan will appreciate it, and you will have a better understanding of your plan.

As noted previously, most plans contain pretty much the same material. Differences involve how the material is structured and what is emphasized. I believe that there's no single "correct" way to do it. Whatever meets the need for you, for your readers, for your organization, for your business situation, and time and resource availability, is correct for you. I emphasize again, that the ultimate objective is to make something happen. You're not writing a novel, but a guide to action. Following are several different outline examples on how to structure a strategic business plan:

- The three Cs approach separates the plan into elements involving — Customers, Competitors, and the Company (i.e., ourselves). All aspects of the plan such as a description and analysis of the current situation, projections into the future, and strategic and tactical intentions are presented on the basis of the 3-Cs. A management summary and financial section completes the plan.

- A different plan arrangement depends on the three Os — Opportunities, Objectives, and Operations. Here we start with the current business situation and look for opportunities and problems. We set objectives aimed at eliminating the problems and taking advantage of opportunities. Operations involves the strategies and tactics to be used to achieve the above, followed by procedures and controls for executing the strategic plan. A management summary and financial section complete the plan.

- For some businesses it makes sense to have a driving force focused plan. Here the emphasis is on one focused area and all the rest is in support of this area. The focus may be a new technology whose mastery will make you or break you. Or perhaps the focus is manufacturing prowess involving output rate, quality, and manufacturing cost. Sometimes the focus is on a process such as competitive advantage through value chain analysis (see Michael Porter's writings), or a portfolio management model as discussed by the Boston Consulting Group and General Electric. Even when you produce a, more or less, conventional plan it's useful to consider the question "What's the single most important element that makes for success or failure in our business?" A financial section and summary completes the plan.

A conventional plan will consist of some or all of the following:

1. A management summary.

2. Business — Beliefs, mission, objectives, definition, policies, primary thrust.

3. Situation description and analysis — Involving markets, competitors, customers, the economy, etc.

4. Assumptions and projections into the future upon which our conclusions are based.

5. Problems, opportunities, strengths, weaknesses, driving forces.

6. Competitive analysis involving the competition's presumed strategies, strengths, and weaknesses; compare these to our own situation.

7. Strategies, tactics, programs, and actions aimed at achieving objectives, taking advantage of opportunities, alleviating weaknesses — all in light of assumptions and current situation analysis.

8. Operations, execution, organization, and resources arrangement that will be used to carry out the plan and achieve the objectives.

9. Controls and performance standards which combined with 8 will lead to successful execution of the plan.

10. Critical issues that we must address no matter what else happens. What are the issues and how we will deal with them.

11. Contingency plans involving a discussion of what can go wrong and what we will do if it does.

12. Budget and resource allocations and needs.

13. Financial results.

14. Appendices involving additional supporting information or some of the above which need not be in the main plan.

- Every type of business, and every specific individual business, needs to be managed to optimize its particular elements of success. Hence the question in a driving force plan — "What is the single most important element that makes for success or failure in our business?"

Remember that savings is the most efficient and productive way of generating a surplus of income over expenses. This translates directly into price and market position flexibility. Drucker (*Managing in Turbulent Times*) identifies four key generic resource elements — capital, physical assets, time, and knowledge.

Which of these, or in what proportion are these key success factors in your type of business? Time-to-market is a key success factor for manufacturers of advanced communication devices, such as pagers and cellular phones. Whoever comes out first with newer features or lower cost devices wins the orders. Time is the critical resource to be managed here. Those who provide the interconnect and transmission service, however, need to manage their physical resources involving cell sites and interconnect switching networks. The greater the capacity loading the better the return on investment. Here the emphasis is similar to the airline business where the essential physical resource is the operating aircraft, and seat capacity utilization is the measure of success. Both businesses follow an incremental pricing strategy with special discounts aimed at filling unused capacity.

You need to determine what it is that makes for success in your type of business, and specifically your own business. It may be, for instance, that knowledge or experience, is a critical element in your type of business and your own essential focus should be on keeping the resident genius happy so she doesn't decide to go elsewhere.

Whatever kind of structure you choose, try to be clear, to the point, and brief. A full fourteen-point plan, as above, could take well over 100 pages. Who has time to study that much material? Stick to the essentials and put the rest in the appendix if you must have it. Stick to a sequence that focuses on actions and needs, rather than conjecture and philosophy. Show your clever reasoning in the appendix for those who are interested. Remember that the purpose of the plan is to make something happen rather than show how clever you are.

4.10 Planning guidelines

I believe that planning should involve as many operating functions, and reporting levels, as is possible to manage without communications paralysis. The quality of the plan, and especially the quality of implementation, is thereby enhanced. But that doesn't mean that each person should go off to do his or her own thing. On the contrary, the more people or departments that are involved in planning, the more important it is to have focus and leadership. This means establishing priorities and operational limits, and providing a common focus by educational means. This focus needs to come either from the group's general manager or an outside source, such as a consultant, brought in by that individual. The material in section 4.8 fits into this general category. Usually, though, the issues deal more with the longer term rather than an immediate emergency.

What follows are excerpts from a strategic planning guide that I was involved with. Some of the material has been modified in order to maintain the anonymity of the organization involved. But most is as presented to the client, a large division, DIV, of a substantial company, COMP.

The material that follows consists of two sections. The first, titled strategic framework, is educational in nature and aimed at fostering a uniform outlook respecting strategy. The second section provides guidance respecting the limits on acceptable strategic positioning. The reader is referred to the writings of Kenichi Ohmae of McKinsey & Co. and Harvard Professor Michael E. Porter for a deeper understanding of many of the ideas presented in this "framework" section.

A Strategic Framework

- DIV is not a new business. It is an established business. COMP expects us to provide an acceptable return to the company. In general, a business needs to earn an average rate of return on its investment in excess of the cost of capital. *Therefore, whatever new products or business that DIV undertakes need to meet financial return requirements.*

- To be successful, DIV needs to be able to profitably sell what it builds. But a firm is profitable only when the price it commands exceeds the cost involved in creating the product. The price depends on the "value" that the buyer perceives. Value is the key to profits, and strategy is the key to value. *Therefore, new products or business undertak-*

ings need to be tested against the existing strategic framework. To pursue a proposal, it's necessary that the proposed endeavor fit within existing strategy or that the strategy be redefined.

- The aim of strategy is to establish competitive advantage, thereby creating superior value. *Proposals for doing something differently or providing new services or products or changing strategy or whatever, need to address and be tested against the notion of improving DIV's competitive advantage.*

- A competitive strategy aims to establish a sustainable profitable position in the business. This can be accomplished by maintaining a competitive advantage within the existing industry segment structure, or by changing the structure. Changing the structure is a bet-your-business strategy. A "dumb" competitor could react in a suicidal manner and kill you along with himself. *Major changes or undertakings by DIV need to be tested against "dumb" competitor behavior.*

- Whatever the strategy, whether focused on a niche segment or aimed at lowest cost or some particular differentiation superiority, it's critical to have one, and to know what your strategy is. Inability to differentiate between strategies or unwillingness to choose one is deadly. You cannot maintain a competitive advantage against a focused-strategy competitor by being all things to all people. DIV's organizational choices need to be based, among other things, on both business and strategic direction. *A new business area involving different customers or technology or whatever, needs to be separated, even if the strategy is the same as for the existing business. Also a new product line within an existing DIV business needs to either follow existing strategy or be separated. If it's not possible to set up a separate group, then we probably should not pursue this product because it will not be successful if it needs a different strategy.*

- A strategy should provide barriers to competitor entry and imitation. A good strategy also provides for easy change or exit. Efficient adaptation to changes is especially important when competing against a leader. It's very important not to attack a strong leader head-on, while a weak follower can be attacked directly. DIV is simultaneously a follower to XYZ and a leader compared to QRS. *We must make sure that our strategy doesn't get us into trouble with either, and provides an advantage against both.*

Strategic Planning Guidelines

DIV is a fully owned subsidiary of CORP, and directly under their oversight. Our owner/banker is looking for the usual things — current return, future survival and growth, good (preferably synergistic) relations with other CORP businesses, good citizenship, etc. Our owner/banker will leave us pretty much alone as long as we provide a good current return and there's confidence in our management, strategy, and organization.

We're supposed to be self-funding after delivering a return to our owner. Our banker is very reluctant to lend us any money. Therefore, it's important that operating costs be aligned with marketplace results in both plan and actual execution.

• DIV business marketplace is currently growing at 15% per year, and projected to do so in the future. DIV is expected to grow at least at that rate, and more likely at 20%. The market share objective is 35% in 5 years compared to 27% now. We get close, at 33%, by growing at 20%/year in a 15% growth market. But the current business plan falls short of this goal given the strength of XYZ at 45% share and the pressure from QRS at 18% share. We need to close the gap between target and plan. Either we find a realistic way to grow faster than the market, or we must convince the owner to remove us from the growth portfolio sector.

• DIV is expected to provide a return in excess of economic break-even. We're looking at a return on invested assets of near 25%[3], and about half that level on sales (2 x asset turns). Don't be surprised if our owner asks for more if we don't offer any growth, per above.

• DIV does not have any undisputed product lines. We are fighting number one, XYZ, and are being chased by QRS. Cost of selling is not likely to diminish. This means that DIV needs to provide a good contribution margin after manufacturing costs. The target is a margin of

---

[3] This is division ROA involving only division assets.

70% of net sales. This translates to 37% manufacturing cost of gross sales.

- The growth goal is very difficult. Our current contribution margin is only 65% and a summation of various costs (sales, technology, etc.) does not fit the profit objectives. Current products will not achieve growth and financial objectives unless XYZ and QRS decide to go out of business. Therefore, we must look to capitalize on new product areas.

- The guideline then proceeds to discuss in detail what has to be done in various new product areas.

4.11 Strategic behavior questions

No two people are exactly alike in life experience, mode of thinking, priorities, or behavior. This can make for a divergence of intentions and other misunderstandings. Yet, to be successful, organizations must work in groups. Hardly anything gets done by a single individual working in isolation. The situation is further exacerbated by differences in mode of thinking and language jargon used by different specialities. The technologist uses words differently than a marketing individual, or financial or human resource specialist. We must be aware that each individual has a personal set of goals which may, or may not, be congruent with organization goals. I've had a dual track career both as a scientist and business manager. I know first hand that it's not a matter of disloyalty or perversity, to badly want to continue a certain line of technology research in spite of the knowledge that it will not really contribute to the business. But sanity usually prevails, because there's a common thread between business and personal objectives. The connection is financial. There's no job if the business fails, and the business fails if there's no income. That's why every individual needs to understand that only one business activity or transaction benefits everybody. That activity is a sale. Only a profitable sale provides income. All other activities and transactions represent an expense. And the only way to have a profitable sale is to provide a price that balances the customer's value against company costs.

Consider the following next time you have a great idea, or someone wants you to support a project.

- Explain in one paragraph what you are trying to do or achieve. Do it in plain language. No special terminology or jargon is permitted.

- Explain how what you will do is different from how it's currently done. Why is it better to do it your way?

- What are the obstacles to success? How will you overcome these obstacles? What resources will it take? How sure are you of success if you get the desired resources?

- So what, and who cares if you do succeed? What difference will it make?

- How long will it take to get a first result?. How long to a final result?

- How will we test interim progress or results? Provide quantifiable measures.

- When and under what conditions will we stop the project and not continue?

There are many other questions, and many other ways of asking questions. Such as:

- Will somebody want to buy this thing at a price we can sell it for?

- Do we have the people skills and organization to build, sell, maintain this thing?

- Can we manufacture it?

- What will the competition do?

- Etc.

Obviously, there's an endless list of possible questions, which means that you can always ask questions to which there's no current answer. Hence, any idea can be easily killed by a judicious choice of questions. That would be foolish. Nothing is without risk, and no one can guarantee success. The purpose of the questions is to generate understanding, test for conviction, exchange information and foster action. Incomplete information from an idea champion who wants to do something is worth more than full information from someone who has no enthusiasm. Remember that the emphasis is on getting something done. Ultimately, the person in charge will have to make a decision somewhat on faith, or intuition actually. The key to overall success is not to be always right — no one can achieve that. Rather, we must strive to quickly recognize when we are wrong, and thus minimize the damage. Taking nothing for granted and always asking questions is a good way to do it.

Chapter 5

Pricing Analysis and Planning

5.1 Analysis and planning

There are numerous ways and levels to price position analysis and price position planning. All of the techniques discussed in sections 2 and 3, as well as the less usual procedures to be introduced in section 6, are applicable. But be careful! You don't want to get into a state of paralysis by analysis. Indeed, one of my concerns in structuring this book has been to provide a full range of information, but not to the point where we lose the forest in the trees. That is one reason why the more basic and essential procedures are presented in section 2, while more advanced concepts are separated into section 3.

Some people routinely use certain concepts with which they are familiar and trust, while ignoring other equally valid ideas. Other people pick what seems to fit a particular situation at any one time. Some people like to go into much detail, while others stop after a minimum effort. My personal style is to do a mini-analysis knowing that it will likely not be enough. From this I usually get a reasonable indication of what the critical or missing issues are, which I then consider in more detail.

Whatever the procedure, the most important part of analysis is to gather information by answering critical questions about your business environment. Two sets of sample questions follow. The first shows an abbreviated analysis structure. You may have to change or ignore some questions to fit your situation, but most should be useful to you. Chances are, though, that these questions will not address all of your concerns, and that you will not be able to answer all of the questions. Even when answered, you will likely feel uncomfortable with the level of accuracy or certainty in many cases. This may force you into some research or to bring in additional people. Whatever the case, you can then proceed to a more detailed analysis.

A detailed analysis deals with a wide range of questions and answers respecting your business situation involving environment factors, such as the overall business, the products, the customers, etc. Before you proceed, however, I suggest that you review the material on process in section 2.1. In particular, remember that the most important questions are human questions, to be answered by a person rather than a computer solving an equation. Once you've satisfactorily answered these questions, then a detailed analytical analysis will help you achieve the desired results.

5.2 Basic analysis

1. Product: Choose and identify a product for analysis.

2. Who's the customer? For example, professional house painters, telephone repair people, accountants, doctors, cancer specialists, people with long hair, people who wear eye glasses, people who have vision difficulties, automobile owners, auto garage mechanics, garage owners. Be as clear and focused as you can. A choice of people with vision problems doesn't have the same implications as choosing eye glass users. The auto mechanic is not the same as the garage owner.

3. What are the important characteristics of this customer as it relates to this type of product? What does this customer care about, or value? Such items could be price, performance features (speed, strength, colors), after sale support, ease of use, how long it lasts, credit terms.

4. List major competing products. This could be direct competition or indirect competition. The competing product could be your own or from a competing company. Your floor tile versus someone else's floor tile is direct external competition. Your carpet versus your floor tile is indirect internal competition.

5. How well does your product fit the customer's needs, wants, and perception of value? Identify by G (good), M (medium), and P (poor).

6. Pick the top four competing products and provide a G, M, and P positioning as in #5.

7. Explain, justify, your answers to #5 and #6.

8. Rank order the five products (yours plus four competing) for meeting customer value. A 1 is best and 5 is worst. What's the rank position for your product.

9. What are the primary factors that establish your position in #8? Better price, less performance, better advertising, etc.

10. Go back to question #4 and rank all products for meeting customer perception of value. Look at the top 5. Are these the same products as in #8?

11. Explain any differences between products in #8 and #10. Do you want to change your mind in your choice of primary competing products?

12. List the price and value ranking of your own and competing products from #11.

Product _____ _____ _____ _____ _____
Price _____ _____ _____ _____ _____
Value _____ _____ _____ _____ _____

13. Compare these products on a price-value basis.

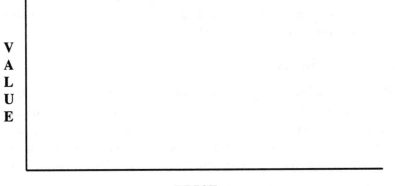

V
A
L
U
E

PRICE

14. How does your product compare to the competition on the price-value plot?

14A. For value. Is that where you want to be? Why? Example answers: Yes, we are satisfied at a lower value because we aim for a very low price. Yes, we want to be at a very high value and charge accordingly. No, we were the highest value until XYZ came out with their product. Now we need to do something about it.

14B. For price, is that where you want to be? Highest, lowest, in the middle? What's preventing you from a price change if you don't like where you are?

14C. How does your price/value ratio compare to the competition. Are you in the upper left quadrant with a high value at a low price? Why are you doing this? Why not charge more and improve profit? Are you in the lower right quadrant with a high price at low value? Why are you so out of line with the competition? Why can't you improve your value, or why can't you charge more price? Do you want to be wherever you are?

15. State your profit objective(s).

16. Has your profit objective affected your product price? How?

17. Do you see any disparity between the price you would like to set based on profit and the price indicated by price-value analysis?

18. List action items. Do you need to get more information, or ask and answer some more questions? Do you need to do something (change price, change advertising...) in order to get the price to where you would like it to be?

5.3 The business

- Explain what business you're in. Not what you sell, but what is your business. If you're in the business of covering floors, then you could (even if you don't now) also deal in carpets as well as ceramic tiles. If you're in the ceramic tile business, then you could (even if you don't now) work with heat resistant tiles for ovens as well as flooring tile.

- Explain why you're in business, and why this particular business. It could be, for example, that this business was started in order to get rich. This looked like a good candidate, but management is willing to do something else entirely if it will provide a superior profit. However, if we're in this business to further an interest in polymer chemistry, then we're not likely to care about the great opportunities in financial services, even though we have every intention to be as profitable as possible in our business.

- List the primary business objectives, and rank order if possible. Examples: Growth, number of employees, help the world (e.g., find food substitutes), be known as the best in?, etc. You must have at least one financial objective such as: make as much profit as possible, or achieve 10% on sales after taxes, or provide minimum profit to stay in business, or return X% on invested capital....

See also 3.17.

5.4 The product(s)

- What product lines and products are offered for sale? Note that a product doesn't have to be a physical item. Whatever we provide the customer for payment, and/or to provide/enhance value, is part of the product. Give a general description by product group or line, in terms of product types in general, and in terms of specific individual products by name or nomenclature.

- Describe the relationship between products (lines). How are these different, how the same, why do we need/have this many? Is the difference in terms of price, quality, performance, customer application? Do we need these to compete against equivalent versions from someone else, to address different market segments, to save cost by changing performance...?

- Product differentiation. What is unique or different about our products vs others, or what is/are unique capabilities that customers want/value: Price, performance, size, service...?

5.5 The customer(s)

- Describe (in general) the customer or user. Examples: Professional house painters, car owners, joggers, hospitals, computer programmers, etc.

- Who determines or establishes the value and makes or approves the purchase? The factory owner, the department head, the computer programmer, the treasurer or controller, the service group... the child who wants the toy or the parent who pays for it... one or another or some of each... How much does each contribute to the value assignment and purchase decision?. Are there important differences for different products or product lines?

- What do the primary, previously identified, buyers value? List the top three to five items in service or performance or financial terms or whatever, that these customers value most. Are there important differences between buyers, product lines, and products?

See also 3.15.

5.6 The competitor(s)

- List and describe your competitors. List companies, divisions, groups. Describe structure, strengths, weaknesses, history, procedures, apparent business objectives, competitive behavior (especially in pricing), align with respect to your business and/or products and/or customers/markets....

- Look at competing products. Which specific competing products (lines) compete against your specific product (lines) and customers? How do these products compare in price, performance, value, image?

- Consider the strategic relationship (see "triangle" 3.14). How does your competitor(s) fit in the strategic triangle? Is this competitor generating much extra cost for you? Is the competitor providing a high level of perceived customer value? Do you cooperate, more or less, or are you at war?

See also 3.16.

5.7 The environment

Describe the market and competitive environment that you now face, and project expectations for the future.

- Consider macro-global issues such as, war, famine, trade disputes, inflation, safety regulations, political issues, environmental and pollution regulations.

- Consider micro-business issues involving the general and specific environment for your own business. You need to look at such factors as new technologies on the horizon, new opportunities in some locations as government alliances change, raw material or supplier issues, cost of capital going up or down.

See also 3.18.

5.8 The segments

- Do you currently segment the market? If not, then develop a segmentation matrix. List the key variables for your segments. The usual variables are product, user/buyer, geographic, distribution. Use as many variables as you have to, to fully describe critical segment parameters, but no more than necessary so as to avoid complexity. The number of segments must be realistic for your business, your industry, your customers. No segments means that you do nothing for everybody. An infinity of segments means that you do everything for nobody.

Set up the matrix and place your products within. Here's an example of a typical segmentation scheme:

	USER/BUYER	RESELLER	INDUSTRIAL	SOPHISTICATED USER
P				
R	bulk/generic	no	yes	no
O				
D	high performance	yes	sometimes	yes
U				
C	large variety	yes	sometimes	sometimes
T				

A 3 x 3 is a small, but workable matrix. A more realistic matrix might show customer types as: East block countries, third world developing countries, pacific rim (e.g., Hong Kong, Taiwan), Europe, U.S.A., Japan. Consider what will happen in the future. Do you want to treat Hong Kong differently after 1997 when it comes under Chinese control, for instance.

- Describe segment characteristics such as, size, growth (past, future), needs, price sensitivity, what do users value, etc.. In what way are the segments different? Are these really different segments? Could some segments be combined? Are some segments too inclusive, and should really be separated into smaller units? Remember that a useful segment involves a group of users or customers who value substantially similar products or services and whose interests and values differ sufficiently from others to be treated differently.

- Position your business or product within the segments. Which are the segments that you primarily serve or compete in? How do you do it — price, performance, service, etc.? Which segments do you not compete in? How well do you meet segment needs, user ideas of value? Should you compete in some segments you are not in because these are linked to other segments?

- Locate the major competitor(s) and their products within segments and analyze as above for yourself.

- Competitor segmentation. You have located your competitor's products within your own segments. Now consider what their own segmentation scheme might be. Construct the segmentation matrix that you think your competitor is using. How well do you fit into this arrangement? How well do you compete? Do you see any danger or opportunities? Do you have pricing opportunities or problems?

- Re-segmentation. Are you satisfied with your market segment situation (i.e,. choice of segments and how you and the competition fit in)? Can you re-segment the market to improve your position? What might the new arrangement be? How do you fit compared to the competition?

See also 3.12 and 7.15.

5.9 The price

- State your general pricing objectives such as to project an image of high value, best price (we will not be undersold), price for growth in sales, price to achieve a stated level of inventory turns, etc.

- Determine the financial and pricing implications of the above. For a credible claim that, "we will not be undersold", our price should be X% below the competition whose price is Y, so our price should be Z. We need X% return on sales to meet our growth objectives without borrowing (see example in 3.24).

- State your financial pricing objectives, such as ROIC or % return on sales. Do this for the business, for product lines, and for individual products.

- Do your prices meet, exceed or fall short of objectives? Explain which products, which objectives and how compared.

- Are you happy where you are, or do you need to make some changes? Yes or no? What do you want these changes to achieve (such as more growth or more % on sales). What are the implications respecting prices?

- Determine how your current prices fit within the customer and competitor environment. For example, Our prices are much lower than the competition, or our prices seem high based on perceived customer value.

- Compare results needs and possibilities. For example: Price results exceed our objectives and compare favorably with customer and competitor positions. We need more profit but prices are already higher than competition. What, if anything, can/might/will we do?

5.10 Profit results

- List profit results such as ROIC, cash flow or % return on sales. Use actual profit results if the analysis is for an existing product. Use expected profit results if the analysis is for a new product.

What is the profit for:

- The product.

- The product line.

- The business or product unit.

- The operating unit or division.

- The company.

• Compare to desired results, objectives and hurdle rates.

• Do you have a profit problem(s)? What is (are) the problem(s)?

• Project future profit results, both quantitatively (give numbers) and qualitatively (describe). What do you expect to happen. Project worst, best, and most likely expectations. Will your profit situation improve or deteriorate? Indicate where, how, when, and why.

• Do you need to change profit results? Current, future or both?

5.11 Price-demand results

Analyze the price and units demand relationship. This is at best a high quality estimate and at worst an educated guess. You have accurate results for only one point, which is your current position. Even this is not available if you're dealing with a new product. It's, therefore, common practice to do a three-point spread to improve the confidence level and provide a sensitivity analysis.

Starting with your current position, marked NOW, fill in the table below, showing expected units volume as the price changes in 5% intervals. Do this three times, using possible maximum volume, minimum volume, and likely or midpoint volume. The product of price times units shows sales revenue. Find the maximum sales revenue for each volume estimate and record as shown.

Price-Demand Chart

VOLUME / REVENUE

		MAX		MID		MIN	
		Q	R	Q	R	Q	R
P	+25%						
	+20%						
R	+15%						
I	+10%						
C	+5%						
E	NOW						
	−5%						
	−10%						
	−15%						
	−20%						
	−25%						

MAXIMUM REVENUE

	Price	Revenue
MAX		
MID		
MIN		

- Do a confidence and sensitivity analysis by considering the following:

  -Will the volume and/or sales revenue change more than you like if you choose the wrong price?

  - How confident are you that the real price-demand relationship falls within the max/min spread? Do it again, if necessary, to get to a 95% confidence level.

  - How big is the max/min ratio? Is it so large that you can't really conclude anything useful? If so, why?

  - What can you, or will you, do to get better information? Do more research if you have to. Continue if you can.

- Plot a price demand graph (see figure 3.1). Try a straight line fit, or several straight line approximations.

- Does the zero-volume price intercept (P_0), where essentially no one will buy, seem reasonable? If not, why not? Can you choose a more likely candidate within the max/min information envelope?

- Consider the zero-price volume intercept (Q_0). Does it seem reasonable? Can you get a better fit?

- Are you satisfied that the demand curve is "real". Are you willing to make serious business decisions based on the shape and slope and position of this graph? Consider, if necessary, alternate market segmentation, a different competitor or product mix, different user value, or price priorities, etc.

Here's an abbreviated introductory example of the procedure. You have determined to an acceptable confidence level (usually better than 85%, ideally 95%) that the P-V relationship is somewhere among the following:

VOLUME / REVENUE

		MAX		MID		MIN	
		Q	R	Q	R	Q	R
P	+25%	65	8,125	75	9,375	80	10,000
P	+20%	72	8,640	80	9,600	84	10,080
R	+15%	79	9,085	85	9,775	88	10,120
I	+10%	86	9,460	90	9,900	92	10,120
C	+5%	93	9,765	95	9,975	96	10,080
E	NOW	100	10,000	100	10,000	100	10,000
	−5%	107	10,165	105	9,975	104	9,880
	−10%	114	10,260	110	9,900	108	9,720
	−15%	121	10,285	115	9,775	112	9,520
	−20%	128	10,240	120	9,600	116	9,280
	−25%	135	10,125	125	9,375	120	9,000

MAXIMUM REVENUE

	Price	Revenue
MAX	85%	10,285
MID	100%	10,000
MIN	112.5%	10,125 *

*Peak revenue falls midway between the 110% and 115% price points

In this example, the current price at 100% is the best probability position within the P-V change envelope. The best price for the elastic, MAX Q change, estimate is at a 15% reduction, or 85% of the current price. We gain 2.85% in sales compared to the current position. But we drop to 95.2% of what we now have if reality is according to the MIN estimate. Similarly, current sales are 1.25% below what could be achieved if the MIN curve is correct. But such a move will lose us over 5% if the MAX position is correct.

A similar analysis can be made with respect to contribution to profit by deducting the product-related costs from the computation. Such an analysis would show that the current price position, which has been optimized for sales revenue, is too low by about one half the product cost.

See also 3.2 and 3.3.

5.12 Contribution to profit

- Do an analysis of contribution-to-profit using whatever relationship fits your business methodology. You might ignore cost and just use ordinary sales revenue (PQ). You could include actual or estimated variable cost (C) and solve for $(P - C) Q$ from the demand curve. Or you can use the straight line approximation and compute maximum contribution at a price of $P = (P_0 + C) / 2$.

  - How sensitive is the maximum contribution profit point to a change in price? Make a graph if it helps you answer this question.

  - Do you have maneuvering room, or do you have to hit the price just right?

  - How does your price compare to the maximum contribution price?

  - Do you have a chance to improve the contribution-to-profit through a price change? What, besides a change in contribution, might happen if you make this price change? Consider such possibilities as a drastic change in volume (impact on capacity utilization), switch of customers to alternate products, switch of product to different segment (hence different demand curve), competitor reaction, etc. Do you still think a price change will benefit you?

See also 3.4.

5.13 Cost components

• Identify the costs associated with this product. There are two ways to do it, by type and by source. I suggest you do it both ways. This will permit a reality comparison between the two results and you will learn a great deal about your business in the process.

Cost contribution by type of cost

- Variable cost, which fluctuates with unit volume.

- Fixed product cost, which does not change with volume, but would not be there if we didn't have this product.

- Other fixed costs and overhead is the cost of being in business.

The sum of the above is the total cost.

Cost contribution by source of cost

- Manufacturing costs, both variable and fixed.

- Marketing costs, both variable and fixed.

- Various other costs, both variable and fixed.

The sum of the above is the total cost.

• Do a reality check. Are the two totals in reasonable agreement? Try to reconcile any disagreement.

• List the primary cost drivers, such as: Purchased materials, loss due to scrap, overtime for extra shifts due to lack of machine capacity, customer training, new technology development, computer services, assembly labor, etc.

• Match cost drivers with specific costs: fixed, variable, manufacturing.

• Estimating costs from income results.

Getting accurate cost information is an almost impossible task. One way to get a cost estimate, and test the reality of other information, is to analyze several months of income before taxes (IBT) results. You can get useful results if you have a reasonably wide range of sales volume and income to look at. Consider the following business results:

Sales revenue (SR)	2,500	4,000	6,000	7,500
IBT	−400	100	1,000	1,400

A best straight line fit to IBT = K (SR) − FC, yields a variable cost slope of about 60% and a fixed cost component (FC) of 1,500.

- Compare the above to a summation of individual cost components. Do results agree? Find the reason for disagreements such as, wrong allocation to product, wrong assignment of fixed vs variable, etc.

- Establish an acceptable variable and fixed cost associated with the product, the product line, and total business. The variable cost is used in contribution analysis from the demand curve. Both, fixed and variable costs are used in break-even analysis.

5.14 Break-even

Do a break-even analysis. (See 3.8 and figure 3.7).

- What sales volume do you have to achieve at the current price in order to break even?

- Assuming no change in fixed or variable costs, what happens to the break-even point and associated profit at different price/volume choices? Use price and unit volume results from the demand curve analysis to plot a family of break-even lines.

Are you better off at a different price than the one you now have? How does that compare to the optimum price you determined from the demand curve?

- Should you change your price? What are the strategic consequences? Perhaps you should follow an incremental strategy and reduce prices after a particular volume is achieved? Consider the consequences, such as competitor reaction or inability to go back to a higher price.

5.15 The experience curve

- How do your current costs compare to future cost expectations based on various environmental factors (such as raw material cost projection) and your experience curve (see 3.9).

- Do you have an opportunity to significantly reduce costs, increase profits or both?

5.16 Perceived value

Answer the following questions about perceived value.

- What value did you assign to your product in market positioning compared to the nearest competitive products?

- What is the value that you "perceive" for your product? Is there a difference? Why? Reconcile any difference.

- What is the perceived value for your product and competitive products assigned by your customers. You should not trust your feelings on this one. It takes market research to properly answer this question.

- Do your customers see you as you see yourself, or as you would like them to see you?

- What are the differences? Why these differences? What can you do about it?

5.17 Price-value comparison

- How do you compare to the competition on a price-value chart (see figure 3.9)?

- Where do you fit on a price-gap matrix (see 2.9)?

- Consider some "what if" scenarios by answering these questions with a different segmentation. What if you compare your product against alternate competing products, or for different markets or different demand curves?

5.18 Pricing strategy

- The purpose of a strategy is to create and maintain a competitive advantage. This means.

  - Create — now.

  - Maintain — into the future.

- Competitive — provide value for your customer.

- Advantage — compared to your competitors.

You need to do this at a price which provides an acceptable (ideally the desired) profit margin. Providing customer value while losing money is usually not considered an advantage.

• Check how well your strategy is working by considering the following:

- Are you providing the value that your customers need or want? If not, then consider how to do it. Can you improve your product offering or perhaps you can reduce the price.

- Do you have an advantage or disadvantage in provided value compared to the competition? Where's the gap? How big is the gap? Think of ways to close the gap if you are behind, or take advantage of the gap if you are ahead.

- Are you meeting your market position objectives in sales revenue, growth, share, etc. Is there a gap? How big and where? What's the primary cause, such as your price, or customer needs, or competitor behavior, etc.

- Are you meeting your profit objectives? Do you need to do something? What possibilities do you have in price, in volume, or in cost changes?

• Consider all essential aspects of your current strategy or of any new strategy you are contemplating. Look at:

- Connection to other products (lines).

- Possibility of shifting to a more favorable demand curve.

- Possibility of re-segmenting the market.

- Bundling or unbundling the offering.

- Gain advantage by creating disadvantage for the competition.

- Don't forget the future. Act now to improve your future position. Test correct behavior for impact on the future.

- Integrate the analysis, actions and strategy. Everything affects everything else. Beware of the law of unintended consequences. Test whatever you decide to do for the possibility that it will make something else worse.

- Close the loop. Why are you in business? What are your ultimate goals? Do you still hold to these now that you know so much more? Consider new goals if the answer is no. Do your chosen actions support your goals?

- Do a backwards reality check. What strategy and objectives would you infer from your pricing behavior if you did not know your plan? How does this compare to your actual plan? Are you sure that your behavior is congruent with your plan? Do you need to change something? What? How?

5.19 New competitor example

We're happily in business, manufacturing and selling lower price/performance product "A", and higher price/performance product "B". We have the following business results:

	A		B		
Price	10		15		
Variable Cost	4		6		
Units volume	1,000		500		
Sales revenue	10,000	+	7,500	=	17,500
Contribution	6,000	+	4,500	=	10,500
Total fixed cost	?	+	?	=	7,500
Profit before tax					3,000
% profit on sales					17.1%

A competitor introduces product "C", with slightly better performance and value than "A", and slightly inferior performance and value than "B", at a price = 12. Our situation has changed to:

	A		**B**		
Price	10		15		
Variable Cost	4		6		
Units volume	700		300		
Sales revenue	7,000	+	4,500	=	11,500
Contribution	4,200	+	2,700	=	6,900
Total fixed cost	?	+	?	=	7,500
Profit before tax					–600
% profit on sales					–5.2%

- Our business has gone from a 17% profit to a 5% loss. What can we do to save the business?

The simplest, quickest and most obvious way to stop losing money is to cut costs. If our business behavior has been sloppy, then there are plenty of places where we can save expenses without affecting the strategic relationship with customers and competitors. This is a very easy idea to understand, but usually very difficult to carry out as it can involve major organizational and procedural changes. Let's assume in this case, however, that we have an efficient business operation and current costs are legitimate. A reduction in costs, then, presupposes also a change in our strategic position. Suppose that profit is the critical factor and we are willing to accept the lower market share strategic position implied by the new volume. Can we find savings due to lower volume?

We investigate the source of the fixed cost (total = 7,500), and find that 2,000 goes for maintaining each separate production line (A&B), and 3,500 comes from being in business. This implies the possibility of a change in strategy involving product line consolidation. Let's investigate the consequences.

I'll assume that we have good historical experience curve information. There are additional complications if we don't. Experience curve information indicates that the variable cost will drop by at least 8% for a doubling of individual product line output. We can expect that variable cost for product "B" will drop to 5.5 at a volume of more than 1000 units, compared to the previous 500 units. This also means that we now have greater losses than we thought, because our cost is higher now that volume is down.

What's the current product "A" sector volume, and what's the demand behavior for this market segment?

We find that people need this item. They will continue to buy even at a reasonable price increase and a price decrease will not significantly increase volume. The demand curve looks inelastic.

We do customer interviews, check competitor serial numbers, look at how many people they employ, etc. We conclude that competition sell 400 units to the product "A" crowd. The entry of product "C" has increased the total sales from 1,000 units before to 700 + 400 = 1,100 now.[4]

• What's the market behavior for product "B"?

Product "B" is a luxury item. Still, people are looking to save money. Our volume dropped from 500 to 300, and an investigation of the competition indicates sale of 400 "C" units to this market. Market size has increased from 500 to 700.

• What can the competitor do if we change products or prices?

We know that they are just starting to learn how to build this product. We know how many people they employ. We have taken product "C" apart so we have parts and construction information. We conclude that they cannot build it for less than our product "B" at a variable cost of 6.

• We investigate their sales volume and decide that they are selling 800 "C" units. We conclude that these go equally to the "A-necessity" market and the "B-luxury" market at 400 each.

---

[4] This increase in volume is not at variance with a relatively inelastic P-V relationship. A new product with new performance features can increase total volume, while a price change for the existing product will not change volume.

- Conclusion: They don't have much room to reduce the price.

Pricing strategy possibility: Remove product "A" from the market and offer product "B" at 12, the same price as product "C".

What will happen to our volume?

- We used to sell 1,000 "A" products. Total "A" market units is now 1,100. The only reason 400 of these use "C", is that "C" is better than "A". Surely at least half of these will switch to the even better "B" model at the same price as "C". We'll gain 200 units.

- Some of the 700 current "A" users will not buy anything. They cannot afford the price increase and/or will be angry at us. Most will get something, though, because this is a necessity market. Our customers tell us that overall they like our service and our company. Product "B" is clearly superior to product "C". Based on the above, we conjecture that 100 of the 700 will no longer buy anything, and 50 more will switch to "C" because they are upset. Our sales to the "A-necessity" segment will be 700 − 150 + 200 = 750.

- The 300 who now buy product "B" will be happy at the price decrease. 100 to 200 of those who now use product "C" will go back to the superior "B", now that the price is down. Another 50 to 100 will join the market at this performance and price. We should be able to attract about 450 product "B-luxury" market users.

Our new financial situation:

Price			12		
Variable Cost			5.5		
Units volume	750	+	450	=	1,200
Sales revenue					14,400
Contribution					7,800
Fixed cost	7,500	−	2,000	=	5,500
Profit					2,300
% profit on sales					16%

The competition is now losing money, and in difficulty. They may have to discontinue product "C" and let us have the whole market. Of course, they might find a way out. Nothing is certain until it happens. What's certain is that we should have been looking at these factors before there ever was a product "C", so as to avoid this problem in the first place.

5.20 Contribution margin example

Financial results have not been good lately. Consequently, you've cut back on fixed costs wherever possible. Promotion and general sales support are two areas that were reduced. Now sales are down, and profit is still marginal. You've asked sales people for advice. The report is unanimous — cut prices by 15%. Sales assures you that unit volume will go up more than the price drop, and sales revenue will increase.

Here's the estimated price-demand result provided by the sales force.

Price %	80	85	90	95	100	105	110	115	120
Units %	130	125	113	106	100	95	88	83	75
Revenue	10,400	10,625	10,170	10,170	10,000	9,975	9,680	9,545	9,000

Clearly, sales revenue is highest at a price of 85%. But that's not sufficient reason to change the price. First you need to discover why profit is so low even though you've reduced costs to the bare minimum. Sure the volume is low, but will more volume increase the profit?

You check and find that the variable cost is at 65% of the sales price. The contribution to profit, remaining after deducting 65% yields:

Price %	80	85	90	95	100	105	110	115	120
Units %	130	125	113	106	100	95	88	83	75
Contribution	1,950	2,500	2,825	3,180	3,500	3,800	3,960	4,150	4,125

The problem is not so much the unit volume as the contribution margin per unit. Clearly, best contribution to profit is at a price increase of 15%, and not a decrease of 15%.

There's now sufficient information to consider what to do. The ideal solution is to reduce the variable cost. A variable cost of 60% yields a contribution of 4,000 at current units. If that's not possible, then a price increase accompanied by reduced sales targets, and/or increased support for the sales effort might yield good profit results. This is particularly true if additional cost savings is available from the reduced volume, such as by closing a currently half empty factory.

Perhaps the solution is in higher volume as considered originally. Lower cost due to bulk purchase of materials or experience curve gains could prove beneficial.

Whatever you do, watch out for unintended consequences.

• Do you really want to close a factory and eliminate jobs?

• Do you really want to reduce the price to increase volume? What if "they" also reduce prices? Your volume will not go up and your profits will go down.

Consider less conventional alternatives before you act: Re-segmenting to move the demand curve, changing the product, bundling or unbundling, etc.

5.21 Commingled segments example

You are the product manager for a product whose direct/variable cost is 50% of price, and fixed costs are 47% of sales revenue. Your manager has told you that the remaining 3% is insufficient to stay in business. You need to improve profit or exit the business.

You decide to examine the possibility of increasing either volume or price. You talk to various people and get a confusing response. Some swear that there is enormous volume waiting for you, if only the price were low enough. Others tell you not to worry about volume. Just raise the price, they say, and all will be well. You spend the effort to get fairly reliable price-demand information, which looks like this:

P	190	180	170	160	150	140	130	120
V	59	63	67	70	73	76	80	86
R	11,210	11,340	11,390	11,200	10,950	10,640	10,400	10,320
Contr.	8,260	8,190	8,040	7,700	7,300	6,840	6,400	6,020
Profit	3,560	3,490	3,340	3,000	2,600	2,140	1,700	1,320

P	110	100	90	80	70	60	55	50
V	92	100	118	158	208	258	283	308
R	10,120	10,000	10,620	12,640	14,560	15,480	15,565	15,400
Contr.	5,520	5,000	4,720	4,740	4,160	2,580	1,415	0
Profit	820	300	20	40	-540	-2120	-3,285	-4,700

Looking at the information you note two sales revenue peaks, one at a price of about 170 and another at a price of 55. No wonder the original information was confusing. The result is indicative of two distinct market segments that place totally different value on the product.

The P-V information, assuming it is reliable, indicates several actions that can be implemented quickly to increase profit.

- Increase the price by about 50% to gain a very substantial profit increase. The demand curve indicates that the optimum price is higher, but demand information is never very accurate. It's best to err on the low side. Too high a price could lose many customers. This strategy means that you are totally abandoning the high volume segment of the business. Do you really want to do this? Better check the implications, such as impact on other products.

- A different strategy is to introduce incremental pricing, if market dynamics and factory capacity permit it. There's no extra profit here on a fully burdened basis, but you do gain a nice contribution to cover fixed costs. This may not work very long, as customers could get used to waiting for a lower price before buying. But incremental pricing could buy time while a more permanent solution is devised.

Various other quick result actions are possible. But before acting, you should consider the implications of selling one product to two markets. A key aspect here, is to realize that serving two different segments hurts your customers as well as your profit. The people who can, and are willing to pay more also want more than you are probably delivering. While the people who are very price sensitive are paying more than they like. Neither segment is fully satisfied. You need to decide what it will take to provide full value to each of the segments.

- What are the critical performance factors that the price sensitive users must have, and what can you eliminate to save cost and price?

- What additional performance factors need to be added to the high price group to really fit their needs and wants, and how much more will it cost?

Analyze the demand curve and restructure into two demand curves, one for each segment (see figure 5.1). Consider the impact of properly serving each segment. You can gain a great deal of units volume at the lower price end, and much price increase at the high price end. An analysis of what would happen might look like this:

- It will cost an additional 10 points to build the product in a way that fully fits the needs of the high cost market. You decide to charge 150 per unit, which is less than the price indicated by the demand curve. You conservatively set the volume at 73, the same as expected for the unimproved model. Conservative assumptions are essential in such a situation, because an error in judgment could destroy the business.

- You will remove some performance the cost conscious group doesn't value much and save 15 variable cost points. You will reduce the price

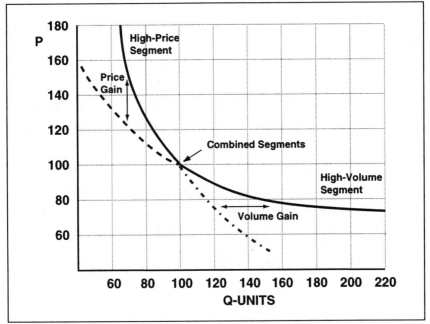

Figure 5.1 Multiple Demand Curve Analysis.

to 70 and assume a volume of 180, compared to 208 forecasted for the unmodified product.

- Setting up an additional product line, and operating at additional volume will increase the fixed cost from 4,700 to 6,000.

The financial result:

	P	V	R	Contribution	Profit
Hi-Volume	70	180	12,600	6,300	
Hi-Price	150	73	10,950	6,570	
Total			23,550	12,870 − 6,000 = 6,870	

The new profit is 6,870 / 23,550 = 29.2%, while before it was only 3%. Furthermore, customers have products much better suited to their needs and wants.

5.22 Product differentiation example

You manage a product which is in the market along with a dozen other competing products of about equal price and performance. It has been an orderly market, smooth and peaceful. Your primary concern has been to assure good product quality, matching output to orders and maintenance of profits.

Quality is critical because your product is installed in a building by a contractor. Ripping it out after installation, if it doesn't work right, would be a serious problem for your customer. You build to order because you can never be sure what color the next order will require. Furthermore, the main office maintains strict inventory level guidelines as a means to maximize cash flow.

Your product related cost is 30% at the current (100%) price, and the contribution to profit is 7,000 points at the current (100%) unit volume. This is safely within the 6,000 point corporate profit contribution target. You manage profit by careful attention to cost of purchased material and control of labor hours. There is very little waste because of good manufacturing quality and you don't buy any material you don't have an order for.

Suddenly your order rate has dropped to 80%. Your contribution to profit is now (100 − 30) (80) = 5600. You no longer meet the corporate target. You investigate for any changes in the market, and the only change you notice is that one competitor is offering an 800 number order-entry service. But their price has gone up by 5%. You investigate some more and find that they are doing very well. In fact, their orders might have actually increased. You don't understand this, because the market is very price sensitive. You decide that the result must be due to their additional advertising to announce the 800 number. You compare their product performance to yours and find it no better, maybe even worse.

You decide to recapture your position by matching the competition. You set your price at 105%, and spend 2% of the increase on major new advertising. You figure that you will easily meet the corporate profit target of 6,000 points because you need only a modest improvement in orders to 83%. Thus: (105 − 32) (83) = 6,059. Unfortunately, the strategy doesn't work. The new advertising doesn't increase order volume, instead volume drops to 70%. Apparently, the market really is very price sensitive as you always thought. The 5% price increase has caused your contribution to profit to decline to only (105 − 32) (70) = 5,110. Your business is now in serious trouble. What's going on here?

The financial situation is even worse than it appears. Obviously, one can construct many scenarios to account for the results. Here's one possibility:

The new 800 order number is not just a minor convenience for the customer. Your competitor promised to deliver the goods by air within four days of a telephoned order, instead of the current industry standard of 14 days. This is based on five days for mail and order entry, five days for shipping and four days for production and processing time. The competitor cut the ordering time from five to one day. Shipping time went from five to one day. And they restructured the factory to go to a three-shift (24 hour/day) operation plus changes to subcontractor material delivery to permit a two-day build processing cycle.

Why should the above have such an enormous impact on orders? Suppose the building contractor didn't get paid until all his work was finished. Suppose further, that your item was the last to be installed, and accounted for only 1% of the total cost. Then: A 10-day difference in delivery is the same as a 10-day difference in waiting for payment. At a 100:1 ratio (you are 1% of total) that's the same as 100 x 10 = 1,000 days, or almost three years. At a money cost of 10%/year, waiting three years to be paid cuts the contractor income value to 75% (see discount table). That's why the contractor is willing to pay an extra 5% to your competitor.

What's the lesson?

- Commodities compete on price. A change in price will have a significant impact on volume. The original market structure was based essentially on equal price and performance products, i.e., commodities.

- Differentiation doesn't have to be based on the product. It can be based on how you do business. Faster delivery moved the product away from a commodity position to a differentiated position.

- Differentiation in an area that's important to the user will provide a competitive advantage. A competitive advantage yields a higher price, higher volume, or both.

- The price to the user is not necessarily the same as the income to the seller. You must determine the true user cost and not just the base sales price when comparing value against competitive products.

Chapter 6
Supplementary Material

6.1 Supplementary material

"Supplementary material" is a polite way of saying that this section contains whatever else I want to say in addition to the previous five sections. This includes various mathematical proofs and formulas, analysis procedures that the reader might find interesting or useful which I believe to be too specialized to fit into a main section, examples of reports or scenarios that illustrate procedures or ideas discussed previously, and so forth. Some of the sections have a common focus, such as the material on demand curve procedures. Other material stands on its own. There's no particular reason or significance to the sequence in which this material is presented. Therefore, there's no particular reason to follow a back-to-front methodology. I suggest that you browse through the section to get a feel for the content then proceed directly to whatever topic might be of interest.

6.2 Demand relationships

I never realized how much material I had collected on the demand relationship — volume related to some other variable — until I started work on this part of the book. I will not burden you with all of it, but much more can be said about demand analysis than has already been presented, such as in 3.2 and 5.11. I believe that the idea of looking at demand volume, not only as a function of price, but also as a function of other variables, such as delivery time, offers a powerful insight into business conditions. Certainly, one can go too far in anything. And it may be that I'm succumbing to a bias in favor of mathematical analysis due to training as a scientist. The cure is simple if that's the case. Use what you like or need and ignore the rest.

The general demand relationship states that the volume demand for a good or a service will vary with change in some other variable, usually taken as price. Thus, you can give many more of something away for free than can be sold at a very high price. All sorts of interesting, and more importantly, useful relationships follow from this idea. The resulting insight can make a significant difference in how to view a business. The problem with this procedure is not the mathematics, which is certainly accurate and generally not very difficult. The problem, rather, is the accuracy of the information that we start with. Demand analysis is a good example of GIGO — garbage in results in garbage out. What's the function of the marketing department, goes a joke. The answer — to guess at the demand curve. And, "guess" really is the correct word. At best all we have is an educated guess. So be careful not to be blindsided by the numbers. But that doesn't mean that such analysis is not useful.

Someone says to raise the price. A look at that person's P-V expectations will tell you almost all you need to know of how this person perceives the market. Knowing that you cannot recover the full manufacturing cost, but only about half of it, is a powerful incentive towards control of costs. You don't need to know the exact demand curve for this. Furthermore, you do have very accurate P-V information at the current market position. So not everything requires a leap of faith. As always, experience and common sense need to be satisfied. A mathematical analysis that doesn't look right is probably wrong. The key point, though, is to discover where or why it's wrong. This will be a question that you would likely not have asked otherwise. Finding a good hidden question is like finding a gold nugget. A bit of work can lead you to a whole new vein of ore you would otherwise not have known about.

6.3 Combined analysis

Break-even, P-V, experience curve.

$$Q(P - VC) = FC + PF$$

Where: Q = units quantity (also volume = V)
P = price
VC = variable cost
FC = fixed cost
PF = profit, PF = 0 @ break-even volume

Examples:

For P = 100%, VC = 50%, FC = 4,000. The break-even volume is at 80% of what it is now. 80 (100 – 50) – 4,000 = 0.

The above procedure works well for a relatively small change in volume, or when price and volume can be considered as independent. A more sophisticated analysis will include demand curve information as shown below:

P %	85	90	95	100	105	110	115
Q %	144	129	116	100	84	70	55
PF	1,040	1,160	1,220	1,000	620	200	–425

The best profit occurs at a slightly lower price than the 100% position we now have.

A linear interpolation shows that the break-even point is at 65 units, not 80 as previously calculated. The difference between 80 and 65 units is big enough to be worth the extra analysis effort. However, to achieve this result calls for a price change. And a price change implies a change in strategy. Hence, 65 units is only a potential break-even point, while 80 units is the actual break-even position based on current pricing.

Why consider a higher price when best profit was shown to occur at a slightly lower price than we now have? Perhaps this product is affecting sales volume of another product which we think could significantly improve in volume (and profit) if this product were priced higher. We're not looking to get rich from this product, because the other one is very profitable. More volume on the other product will more than make up the difference. We cannot eliminate the first product because our customers demand it. So we decided to sell it at a break-even price and concentrate volume production on the second product. A 5% to 10% price increase looks pretty safe from this analysis.

The above shows how a combination of demand and break-even information yields a lower break-even point by use of a price increase. Combining demand with experience curve learning, yields a lower optimum price than might otherwise be considered.

A highly elastic demand, where volume is very influenced by price, when combined with a high rate of cost reduction due to experience curve learning, yields a result that can be likened to a perpetual motion machine. You get good profits at zero price and infinite volume. This means that you control the whole market and no competitor can ever bother you. Consider the following relationships:

- Let price times volume equal sales revenue, and let the volume vary inversely with price such that revenue is constant: $R = PQ$.

- Let learning from experience cause the variable cost to change inversely with volume: $VC = K / Q$.

- Then: Contribution to profit is $CPF = Q (P - VC)$. Substituting that $Q = R / P$ and $VC = K / Q$, the result is that contribution to profit is just $CPF = R - K$ regardless of price.

The above cannot happen in real life. But certainly, factoring in experience curve savings can make an important contribution to pricing strategy. Consider the following, more realistic, example:

- Your price now is $P = 100$. Your volume now is $Q = 100$. Variable cost now is $VC = 50$. Then, contribution to profit is:

  $CPF = 100 (100 - 50) = 5,000$.

- Demand information shows that a 30% reduction in price, to $P = 70$, will double the volume to $Q = 200$. This is very attractive as it will keep the competition out of this market. But that means a reduction in contribution to profit to $200 (70 - 50) = 4000$.

Suppose, however, we have a 20% experience curve gain on costs every time the volume quantity is doubled. Then, the cost goes to $50 (0.8) = 40$. The actual contribution to profit is $200 (70 - 40) = 6,000$. Not only did we capture more market share, but the contribution to profit has actually increased.

There are examples in the literature of spectacular success stories based on such a strategy. There are also plenty of examples on spectacular failures. You are, in effect, betting your business that the volume will increase as predicted when you reduce the price, and that your cost will decrease as predicted when you increase the volume. An error in one or the other of these assumptions and you might never recover.

6.4 The P-V tangent relationship

For a demand relationship involving volume = Q units, at a price of P per unit and variable cost per unit of VC, the contribution to profit is given by $CPF = Q (P - VC)$.

Let the relationship between P and Q be of arbitrary curvature asymptotic to both price and volume, described by the equation:

$$Q = Q1 (P / P1)^{-n}$$

Where: Q1 and P1 are the volume and price at which we choose to be (see figure 6.1).

Combining with the relationship for contribution to profit we get:

$$CPF = \frac{Q1P^{(1-n)}}{P1^{-n}} - \frac{Q1VCP^{-n}}{P1^{-n}}$$

Differentiating CPF versus P, and setting equal to zero in order to find the price that provides highest contribution to profit, we get:

$$\frac{(1-n) Q1 P^{-n}}{P1^{-n}} + \frac{nQ1VC P^{-n-1}}{P1^{-n}} = 0 \; ; P(max) = \frac{nVC}{n-1}$$

For a straight line demand relationship with price and volume intercepts at P_0 and Q_0, we have:

$$Q = -Q_0 P / P_0 + Q_0$$

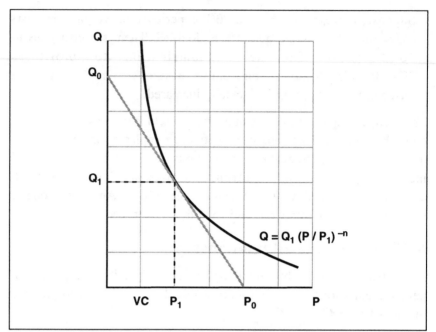

Figure 6.1 P-V Curve for Contribution-to-Profit Derivation.

Substituting into contribution to profit equation, we have:

$$CPF = -Q_0 P^2 / P_0 + Q_0 P + Q_0 PVC / P_0 - Q_0 VC$$

Differentiating CPF versus P and setting equal to zero to find the price P(max) that yields a maximum CPF, we have:

$$-2Q_0 P / P_0 + Q_0 + Q_0 VC / P_0 = 0.$$

This yields:

$$P(max) = (P_0 + VC) / 2.$$

For a straight line P-V relationship, the maximum sales revenue involving the area under the triangle (R = PQ) occurs at a price of Po / 2.

Conclusion: *We can only recover half the impact of variable cost by a VC / 2 price increase.* A full VC price increase will yield less profit.[5]

---

[5] Even the one half recovery is not complete as the new contribution peak is smaller than the maximum contribution without the cost.

Let the straight P-V line be tangent at the point P_0, Q_0. Then:

$(Q1 / P1) n = Q_0 / P_0; P_0 = P1 (1 + n) / n$

Hence:

$$P(max) = \frac{P1 (1 + n) / n + VC}{2}$$

$$= \frac{VC [n / (n-1)] [(1 + n) / n + VC}{2}$$

$$= \frac{nVC}{n - 1}$$

The result for the straight line tangent and for the arbitrary P-V curve are identical provided we stay near the original position at P1, Q1. Therefore, it's appropriate to use a straight line simplification for small price adjustments or fine tuning a pricing strategy. A major price change usually calls for a complete reconsideration of strategy, segmentation, and P-V demand shape.

6.5 Contribution to profit

It was shown that for a straight line P-V relationship, the price for maximum contribution to profit is $P = (P_0 + C) / 2$. Thus, the statement in section 6.4 that we can only recover half the impact of variable cost by a $C / 2$ price increase. This might imply that we get back half the impact on profit. But, it's not so. The impact on profit, or contribution to profit to be more precise, is more severe. This is because we are hurt twice — once by the fact that we cannot increase the price by the full value of C, and once by the fact that the volume quantity is reduced as we increase the price by $C / 2$. The loss in contribution does not follow the change in price. In the example below, the price change is 1 out of 6, or 17%, but the contribution is reduced by approximately half the cost change. A cost change from 2 to 4 is 100% and the impact on contribution under ideal conditions is 44%. Hence, the new maximum contribution to profit due to a cost increase is quite a bit lower than one might expect. For example, for a straight line P-V relationship with $P_0 = 10$ at zero volume, and $Q_0 = 100$ at zero price:

P	1	2	3	4	5	6	7	8	9	10	
Q	90	80	70	60	50	40	30	20	10	0	
CPF	–	0	70	120	150	160	150	120	70	0	(C = 2)
CPF	–	–	–	0	50	80	90	80	50	0	(C = 4)

When the cost is $C = 2$, the maximum contribution to profit is 160 at a price of 6. This is in agreement with $P = (P_0 + C) / 2 = (10 + 2) / 2 = 6$. The maximum contribution to profit drops to 90 at a price of 7 when the cost is increased to $C = 4$. This is a loss of $160 - 90 = 70$ points to profit out of an original 160, or over 40%. And to get there, it was necessary to increase the price from 6 to 7. Frequently, it's not possible to increase the price when the cost goes up. Remember that your customer is paying you for value and not for your cost. Had the price remained at 6, then a cost increase from 2 to 4 will yield $(6 - 4)\ 40 = 80$ points to profit and not 90. Even when a cost increase is possible, it usually takes time and there are costs associated with the procedure, such as a need to change literature and educate sales people and customers as to the change.

Even under ideal conditions, where an instantaneous price change is possible, the impact on profit from a cost increase is significant. How much the impact is, however, is difficult to estimate from examples such as above. We can get a better insight by developing a direct equation by combining the basic relationships. A little mathematical manipulation of:

$$Q = -(Q_0 P) / P_0 + Q_0, \quad P = (P_0 + C) / 2, \quad CPF = (P - C)\ Q$$

Yields:

$$CPF = Q_0 / 2\ (P_0 / 2 - C + CC / 2P_0)$$

We find from this equation that at $P_0 = 10$, $Q_0 = 100$, and $C = 2$, the maximum contribution to profit is:

$$CPF = 100 / 2(10 / 2 - 2 + 4 / 20) = 160$$

This is as found previously by direct calculation. Using this equation, we can substitute different values of C to test for the sensitivity of the contribution to profit as a function of costs.

Another variation on the above CPF versus cost relationship is to look at what happens as cost changes with respect to price. Cost can never be permitted to exceed price as that leads to a loss. In the other direction, cost cannot be less than zero. Thus, at zero cost, all of the sales revenue is a contribution to profit. When cost equals the linear P-V price intercept, P_0, we get zero contribution to profit. These statements are represented by $C = kP_0$. Cost is zero when $k = 0$ and cost equals the zero volume price P_0, when $k = 1$. A substitution into the CPF equation shows that:

$$CPF = Q_0 / 2 \, (P_0 / 2 + k \, (kP_0 / 2 - P_0))$$

From the above we can compute how much of the sales revenue contributes to profit as a function of k, which varies between 0 and 1:

k	0	0.1	0.2	0.3	0.4	0.5	0.6	0.7	0.8	0.9	1.0
CPF % OF REV.	100	81	64	49	36	25	16	9	4	1	0

We note that a critical issue is not so much the magnitude of the cost, but on how cost compares to the maximum possible price. Clearly, the best possible CPF drops drastically as the cost becomes an appreciable percentage of the price. Cost cannot be eliminated entirely. There's always a cost associated with a sale. But the manager must make every possible effort to keep costs at a minimum. Cost reduction is a very powerful profit enhancer.

6.6 P-V with competition

General market research deals with overall users of an item, and the price-demand relationship applies to the whole market. Hence competing products are included. Your product only has a share of this market. Reasonably accurate P-V information for the total market can be very important in establishing a business strategy. Ultimately, though, it's useful to consider how the market reacts to just your product. Sometimes it's possible (through brand loyalty studies or where you are the dominant supplier, for example) to directly establish a P-V relationship exclusively for your product. What if you cannot do this?

First you need to establish how your products will do against the competition as a function of price. This involves a market share, rather than units volume, versus price demand relationship. The simplest analysis is based on a fixed and unchanging market size. This is applicable if you are a very small part of the total market, or your price change will be very small. Otherwise, a change in your price will also change the size of the market, even if the competition does nothing. Fortunately, if you are big enough to significantly modify the total market, you are probably able to to get direct information for an exclusive P-V relationship.

Find the product of the two demand relationships, P-V for market including competitors and P vs share for your product, to yield a single product P-V curve.

It's useful to have "share" demand information even when full P-V demand is available. How your price affects share will give you an idea of competitive reaction to a price change, for example.

Consider the following hypothetical example. You believe that you now have a 20% market share. This could mean that you are the dominant supplier compared to 30 other, smaller, competitors, or perhaps you are a junior player compared to number one who has 70% share, or whatever. The issue of comparative size is beyond the scope of this analysis. Anyway, you now have a 20% share and a market study leads you to believe that your share will change as a function of your price, as follows:

Price %	80	90	100	110	120
Share %	24	22	20	18	16
Relative units %	120	110	100	90	80

You've established that the total market P-V is given by:

Price %	80	90	100	110	120
Market units %	130	115	100	85	70

Taking the product of the above two demand curves yields the P-V relationship for your product, provided your behavior doesn't disturb the total market and your competitors don't react to what you do.

Price %	80	90	100	110	120
Your units %	156	126.5	100	76.5	56

This is a highly elastic demand. A small change in price causes a significant impact on your units. Are you confident that the market will really behave this way? Perhaps this is the most elastic among several market demand estimates. Let's see what happens for a less elastic situation.

Price %	80	90	100	110	120
Market units %	110	105	100	95	90

The P-V result for your product shows:

Price %	80	90	100	110	120
Your units %	132	115.5	100	85.5	72

You have a zero-sum market when the market is totally inelastic. Any change in your units as a function of price has to result in a change in units for the competition. This makes it more likely that a competitor will react to your behavior. A highly elastic market, on the other hand, permits a change in results for you with less of a disturbance for your competitor. Hence you have a better chance of not getting a competitive reaction. Whether you decide to make a price change, how much and what sort of advertising you use, etc. depends on your share and P-V demand relationships and who has a dominant market position, you or a competitor.

6.7 P-V with cost

The price-volume demand curve can be combined with other information for a more sophisticated analysis.

People who believe in a high volume at low price strategy will look at a combination of P-V with the experience curve. This is because: The more you sell, the more you build. The more you build, the more experience you have. The more experience, the less the cost. The less the cost, the less you can afford to charge. The lower the price, the more you sell, etc.

An incremental pricing strategy will benefit from an analysis that combines break-even information with the P-V curve.

Here I consider the combination of P-V information with cost distribution and/or cost allocation information in an examination of how to obtain best % return or best absolute profit.

First, we separate cost items on the income statement into fixed or variable. Some costs can be both. For example, our product sells for $7,500/each, and we sell 100 per year for $750,000 total yearly revenue. The manufacturing cost of sales per unit is $2,500. There are other semi-variable costs, such as sales commission, that come to 32% ($2,400 / units @ P = $7,500). The total fixed cost is $185,000. This yields an absolute profit of 100 (7,500 − 2,400 − 2,500) − 185,000 = $75,000, and 75 /750 = 10% return on sales. Note that the above is a simplified situation that ignores the impact of discounts, net vs gross sales, taxes, etc.

Imagine that you have developed what you believe to be reasonably accurate P-V information. Total sales revenue is the product R = PQ. The profit is computed from PR = Q [(1 − 0.32) P − 2,500] − 185,000. The return on sales, or percent profit (%PR) is the ratio of profit to revenue.

P	6.0	6.5	7.0	7.5	8.0	8.5	9.0
Q	134.0	122.0	111.0	100.0	89.0	78.0	67.0
R	804.0	793.0	777.0	750.0	712.0	663.0	603.0
PR	26.7	49.2	65.9	75.0	76.7	70.8	57.4
%PR	3.3	6.2	8.5	10.0	10.8	10.7	9.5

It appears that a price of $8,000 is optimum for both absolute profit ($76,700) and for percent return on sales (10.8%). But we need to be cautious. P-V information is never certain. What if we're slightly off? The drop in profit appears to be quite significant as the price goes below $7,500 and above $8,000. Even if $8,000 is better than $7,500, it's not better by much. Consider the cost of changing the literature, notifying customers, changing the order entry system. We need to look at this more closely.

Ideally, a closer look at this situation involves getting more accurate demand information. But that's probably not available. The next best thing is to adjust the existing P-V numbers to check for sensitivity to change. Namely, how much does the best price move as we go to a more elastic and to a less elastic demand curve.

The more elastic case:

P	6.0	6.5	7.0	7.5	8.0	8.5	9.0
Q	160.0	140.0	120.0	100.0	80.0	60.0	40.0
R	960.0	910.0	840.0	750.0	640.0	510.0	360.0
PR	67.8	83.3	86.2	75.0	50.2	11.8	loss
%PR	7.1	9.2	10.3	10.0	7.8	2.3	

The less elastic case:

P	6.5	7.5	8.5	9.5	10.0	10.5	11.0	11.5	12.0
Q	110.0	100.0	90.0	80.0	75.0	70.0	65.0	60.0	55.0
R	715.0	750.0	765.0	760.0	750.0	735.0	715.0	690.0	660.0
PR	26.2	75.0	110.0	132.0	138.0	140.0	139.0	134.0	126.0
%PR	3.7	10.0	14.4	17.4	18.4	19.0	19.4	19.4	19.1

A more elastic market wants a lower price and a less elastic market calls for a higher price. This is the usual situation for any P-V analysis. There's no need for detailed calculations here. However, the detailed calculations also show that the sensitivity is not the same in both directions. The maximum occurs at a price of $7,000 for the elastic market compared to the original price of $7,500. For the inelastic situation, however, the best profit is at a significant price increase to $10,500. And best percent return is at a price of $11,000.

Ideally, this dilemma could be resolved by obtaining more accurate P-V information. Unfortunately, this is easier said than done. An alternative is to investigate the market P-V relationship from a different point of view and compare to the assumptions made in constructing the original demand curve.

We know one point on the demand curve perfectly, namely at P = $7,500. This is the usual starting point for constructing a demand curve. Talking to customers and sales people and checking for market behavior of similar, but differently priced, products yields an expectation of P-V behavior in the vicinity of our starting point. The more we deviate from P = $7,500, the more the likely error. Fortunately, the original P-V analysis ranged only over a 20% price change, from $6,000 to $9,000 with $7,500 as a starting point. The same range was used for the elastic market variation. This was sufficient to find the optimum price in both cases. Not so for the inelastic variation. Here it was necessary to extend the price to $12,000, a 60% change from the starting point at $7,500.

The continuation of the demand graph beyond a price of $9,000 isn't based on any new information. It's simply an extension of what was used before, at the rate of 10 units change in volume for a $1,000 change in price. Is this realistic? It doesn't take very much research to discover the highest price at which customers will consider any purchase at all. Suppose this happens to be $12,000? We know, then, that the P-V relationship must drop off to near zero volume at P = $12,000. This provides information for a more realistic P-V relationship at higher prices.

P	6.5	7.5	8.5	9.0	9.5	10.0	10.5	11.0	11.5
Q	110.0	100.0	90.0	85.0	75.0	65.0	50.0	30.0	5.0
R	715.0	750.0	765.0	765.0	713.0	650.0	525.0	330.0	58.0
PR	26.5	75.0	110.0	123.0	112.0	94.5	47.0	loss	loss
%PR	3.7	10.0	14.4	16.0	15.7	14.5	9.0		

Now we have some results that we can compare:

	original P-V	elastic P-V	inelastic P-V
P @ max profit	$8,000	$7,000	$9,000
P @ max %	$8,000	$7,000	$9,000

The best price for absolute profit and percent return on sales is the same in all cases. There was no need for the additional calculation. Could we possibly have saved some work on the other detailed calculations? Yes, by using the straight line approximation. The zero volume intercept price is $P_0 = \$12,000$. Then: The best result based on a variable cost of $2,500 is (12,000 + 2,500) / 2 = $7,250. The best result including other variable costs of $2,400 is at (12,000 + 2,500 + 2,400) / 2 = $8,450. Using 32% of price, rather than $2,400 for the other costs, yields P = (12,000 + 2,500 + 0.32P) / 2 = $8,630.

The direct and straight line analyses are in fairly good agreement that the optimum price is somewhere around $8,000. We could have saved some work by going to the straight line first. But that would not provide the confirmation, and confidence to act that comes from getting a similar result from several methods. My advice is to do it the easy way if you are just thinking about it. But do the extra work to compare results with different methods if you are serious about making a change. It's very difficult and costly to recover from a mistake.

6.8 Demand vs delivery and demonstration

The price-demand relationship is well established in marketing practice. The theory states that the order quantity is a function of price. Similar relationships can be developed, such as demand as a function of delivery time (T) or number of demonstration units (U).

Obviously, as T increases, a point will be reached where customers will no longer be willing to place orders that far in advance. Therefore, orders go to zero as T goes to infinity. Similarly, for certain products, it's difficult to get an order without showing the product in advance. We need to have some demonstration units on hand. Eventually all who want to see the product can do so. A further increase of demonstrator units will have no effect.

Demonstration units increase assets and decrease profits. Ideally we would like to have none. But that will not work if it significantly depresses sales. A fast delivery of a costly specialized item also reduces profits. Either we must pre-build, or invest in a system that provides a very fast response to orders. In either case, an analysis of impact on sales can be useful. Unfortunately, very little practical information is available from which to construct the graphs. However, even a very approximate graph will provide useful information. The graphs that follow were constructed by the author for a costly and complex industrial item.

- **Demo units.** The graph is based on orders information as demonstration units were added to a new product introduction. The data is clearly

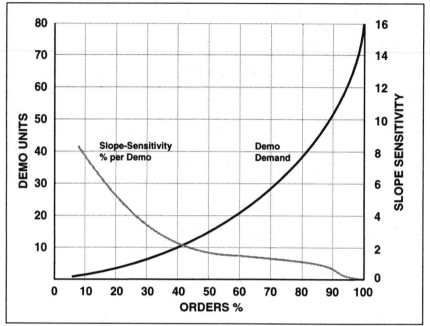

Figure 6.2 Demo-Demand Analysis.

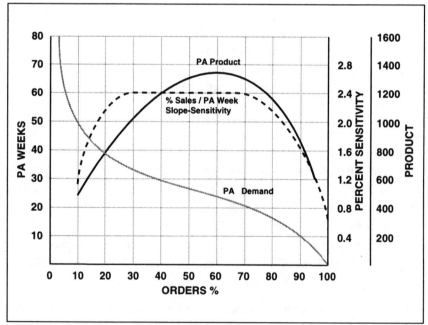

Figure 6.3 Product Availability vs Demand.

Supplementary Material

flawed as many factors besides an increase in demonstrators have an impact over time. Product recognition as a result of advertising is one such factor, for example. Nevertheless, the result is better than nothing.

For the chosen territory. Taking the units quantity order rate with no dearth of demonstration units at 100%, we found a 5% order rate with zero demonstration units. The first demonstration units were carefully controlled to go to high potential customers. Orders per demo unit were high. As more demonstration units were added, the order rate per demo unit went down somewhat and held constant until all well-qualified customers could see the product at any time. A continued increase in demo units showed a decrease in orders per demo, as demo units went to marginal customers or were not used at all.

The result of the above is shown in figure 6.2.

- **Delivery time**. The graph is based on a product that had delivery problems after public announcement. Only 10% of users were willing to place an order with a one year product availability (PA). The order rate improves at a pretty much linear rate as delivery time decreases to 15 weeks. The impact of delivery time on orders is progressively lower as delivery time goes to zero.

The result of the above is shown in figure 6.3.

- **Derived graphs.** One useful derived result shows sensitivity of demand. This shows the sensitivity, or change in demand, for a small change in delivery time (T), or a small change in demonstration units availability (U). The sensitivity graphs show the slope of the demand curves.

Another interesting relationship involves the product of order rate and delivery time. This is equivalent to the sales revenue result computed as the product of price and order rate.

- **Interpreting the graphs.** The product of time and order rate shows a peak at 60% of maximum order rate at a 23 week delivery time. To the extent possible, we need to keep delivery time to less than 23 weeks.

The delivery sensitivity curve shows a plateau at 2.4% order-change per one week of delivery time. A small change in delivery time does not do very much when delivery time is long and the order rate is low. Likewise, delivery time is not critical when delivery time is low and the order rate is high. In the middle, though, a small change in delivery time has a substantial impact on orders. It's important to push delivery time to the low-end corner if orders are to be maintained. Expanding much energy or resources to go below the sensitivity corner, however, may not be worth the effort. The best place appears to be between 23 weeks and 15 weeks. Going above the upper sensitivity corner at 37 weeks means trouble.

The sensitivity of orders versus demonstration units shows a sharp change in slope at about 10 demo units. This should be the minimum acceptable number. Depending on manufacturing output capacity, ability to sell used products, and asset turn needs, it may be useful to have up to 40 demonstration units. A further increase generates only a marginal impact on orders.

- **Strategies.** Here we are in unknown territory. My analysis is purely hypothetical as I've assumed that delivery time and demo unit level are independent variables for the same product. I've also assumed that we can use the same procedure for either a new product or an established product.

  1. Production output for an established product should equal the order rate called for by the chosen delivery time and demonstrator level. Demonstrator level should not exceed the flat part of the sensitivity curve at 40 units and 85% of maximum orders, unless you are in very great need of more orders. Delivery time need not be much less than the sensitivity curve corner at 15 weeks and 80% of possible orders. The order rate will be 0.85 x 0.80 = 0.68 of the possible maximum.

     What happens if our production capacity is only at the 60% level? Then delivery time will increase and the order rate caused by delivery will decrease to 0.71 (0.71 x 0.85 = 0.6). From the delivery demand curve, this represents an 18 week waiting time. But wait a moment. The sensitivity curves show that one week of delivery time yields 2.4% of orders, and one demonstrator unit is worth 1.3% of orders. Therefore, we can reduce demonstration units by 6, maintain delivery at 15 weeks, and end with the same orders. As a result, our return on assets is improved because of a lower inventory level.

2. The first requirement in planning the behavior for a new product is to decide where we want to end up. Suppose the business plan, growth, cash flow, or whatever criteria, dictate a stable position at 50% of saturated (100%) sales. Suppose further that this is 260 units per year, or 5 units per week (100% is 10 units per week). We can get there several ways. Here's one example:

We want to operate at the lowest demonstrator quantity level. Hence, delivery is at the upper sensitivity knee representing 15 weeks at 80% of maximum sales. This calls for 62.5% sales and 23 units on the demonstrator curve (0.625 x 0.8 = 0.5). This represents less than 5 weeks of production output at a 5 units per week rate. A guaranteed delivery of 15 weeks, with 5 weeks worth of output used for demonstrators, calls for product announcement not more than 10 weeks prior to first manufacturing output.

6.9 Entering established market

It's generally difficult to enter a well established market and capture market share. Usually, the user feels comfort in the familiar product, and the established competitor has worked hard to establish brand loyalty. To be successful the new entrant will need to provide something new, better, or less costly than previous suppliers. Whatever it is, you will not succeed unless you convince the customer that switching will provide greater "value". Hence it's important to understand what the customer values, and what level of value premium can lead to a sale for you. Here are three examples of possible market dynamics:

General use customers are willing to switch products but are not eager to experiment. Usually, you will not get any attention unless your price is below a perceived threshold of what is acceptable. Once the price barrier is satisfied, though, you can usually compete on the basis of other factors such as performance, ease-of-use, durability, service, and so on. The demand curve is the same for you as for the established competitors, but your product needs to prove its "value" first. It will take additional advertising, free samples, or whatever to get users to try your product. But after that you'll have a "fair" chance to compete.

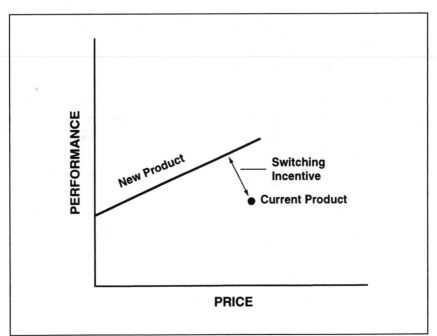

Figure 6.4A Fixed-Position Switching Incentive Plot.

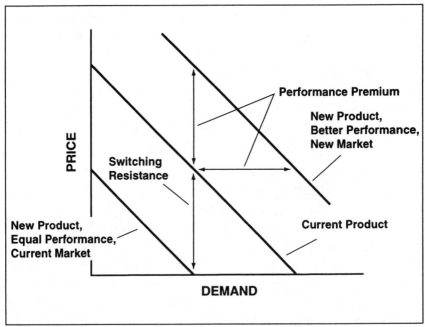

Figure 6.4B Demand-Style Switching Resistance Plot.

Supplementary Material

A value based market will switch and mix products at will to find the best "value" mix. These people will look for best price, performance, service or whatever to get a best price to performance value ratio. This is a textbook demand curve market and you have as much opportunity as anybody else to do a better job and win the sale.

Unfortunately, the new entrant frequently faces a **repeat user market**. These people have been using a certain product, or products, for some-time. The user has invested significant financial and emotional capital in this choice. Familiarity, comfort, safety, prior documentation, etc. are all anti-switching factors. Switching resistance is high, except in those instances where the original choice was clearly deficient. The switching price differential may be 30% or more. Indeed, you may not be able to give it away for free when dealing with installed equipment or machinery. The cost of learning how to use the new item may be greater than its price. It's almost impossible to overcome resistance to switching by means of price for a equal performance item. Only an item that is perceived to be somewhat of a clone in physical and operating features has a chance to win on the basis of a reasonable price difference. The major opportunity to win is with a product that's perceived to be substantially better in some important attribute at a competitive price.

The above market behavior is illustrated in figures 6.4A and 6.4B. Figure 6.4A shows a fixed volume relationship between the current and newly introduced products. It takes a substantial performance or price and performance incentive to overcome switching resistance. You need to do market research to determine what sort of performance, and what level of price and performance, it will take to get a reasonable chance at a sale. Figure 6.4B is a multiple P-V graph of the same type as figure 3.6. A new, equal-performance product, has significantly lower quantity potential than a product already well established in the current market. A new, higher-performance product, will eventually reposition the market to a higher level P-V line once the new product penetrates the market. But in the meantime you need to overcome the switching resistance illustrated in figure 6.4A.

6.10 Income statement

Profit, or earnings, is what's left from your income after you've paid expenses. This is represented in the income statement by the simple relationship: Earnings = net sales – cost of goods sold – other expenses – taxes. Unfortunately, this very simple formulation, is only usable for a very simple business. Two problems get in the way: timing of transactions and complexity of transactions and business structure. Therefore, the determination of earnings involves quite a complicated set of calculations, as shown below. Furthermore, for a division subset of a larger business, it's possible to choose — dare I say manipulate — the statement structure to emphasize one or another result. Certainly, there are accounting standards to be maintained and there are legal requirements aimed at preventing investor fraud and proper tax payment. But even if these controls were perfect, which they aren't, we would still have the substantial problems involved in intra-company transactions such as allocations to divisions for use of corporate assets or intra-divisional cost of goods transfer prices. It's easy here to lose sight of the forest on account of the many trees. Try not to let this happen to you. Whenever possible, try to combine or eliminate the intermediate issues and get to the only point that really counts: all income less all expenses equals all earnings. The discussion of details that follows is aimed at helping you get to this fundamental result.

- **Accrual accounting.** One complication in using the income statement involves timing differences among transactions. A small and simple business can operate on a cash basis. Revenue and cash become almost synonymous. Income is counted when you are paid, and an expense is counted when you pay. Your checkbook register can almost act as an income statement. Such an income statement not only shows the result of an accumulation of income over time, but also the instantaneous state at some particular time. Not so for any reasonable sized business. Here, transactions don't wait to be recognized until paid, but are recognized when payment becomes a legal expectation. This is known as accrual accounting. You send a bill out and it's recognized as income, even if it takes 45 days before you see any money. Your income statement may show good earnings, but you might have to borrow to cover your payroll. Eventually, everything does balance out over time. An income statement for the year will give a fairly accurate representation of your business results. Furthermore, a year-to-year comparison will show how the business is progressing.

Income statements are, however, also used to look at profits for the quarter, for the month, and sometimes even for one week. The shorter the time period the more misleading the result. Suppose, for example, you've pulled off a great coup and beaten the competition to a very large products order. Part of the agreement involves a guaranteed delivery date. You're certain that the business is yours and, in order to meet delivery, you set up a new production line to build the product. By accrual accounting, the invoice to you for these costs will be recognized, maybe months, before income is recognized from the sale. On the books, it looks like you did a terrible job because your business shows (temporarily) a loss.

- **Gross or net sales.** Timing mismatch due to accrual accounting can obscure the real state of a business, as in the above example. But it can be dealt with fairly easily. Don't use the income statement as a management tool for short time differences, and add an explanatory note where appropriate. But problems due to income and expense identification are much more difficult to deal with. This area is particularly problem prone in a multi-division organization. Distribution of profit and expense among divisions, and cost allocation for centralized functions can make life confusing and difficult for division management. This book is not a treatise on financial management, nor do I claim particular expertise in the field. But every manager, no matter what job designation, has to understand some things. Otherwise, you might go out of business as shown in the costing example given in section 3.6.

The usual starting point on the income statement (IS), also known as a consolidated income statement or income and expense statement, is net sales revenue. This is determined by deducting discounts and other adjustments, such as an allowance for uncollected invoices, from gross sales. These deductions are to a large degree under the control of the business manager. Hence, for business management purposes it's recommended that gross, rather than net sales, be the starting point. Normally, selling costs will appear in the other expense section of the IS.

Frequently though, this will appear as a discount from gross to net sales to an outside selling representative or transfer price adjustment to an international subsidiary. Total earnings will not be affected, but percent of net sales earnings will be. For example. $1,100 (gross) – $100 (discounts) = $1,000 (net) – $400 (mfg cost of goods) – $500 (other expense) = $100 (earnings). We have 10% earnings for $1,000 in net sales. Suppose that $150 of the $500 (other expense) is the selling cost of a subsidiary. Showing this as a discount will reduce net sales to $850, and increase earnings to 11.8% of net. But nothing has changed in the business. Sales, costs, or income has not changed. Yet, a change in how we designate an expense affects the final result. I'm not going to tell you that one formulation is better, or more correct, than the other. I do believe, however, that it's not sufficient to look at just net results. You need to know how you get from gross to net.

- **Cost identification.** The usual procedure respecting costs, is to separate the cost of producing what you sell from all other costs. This presumably distinguishes between the necessary costs of building what you sell and other, more discretionary, costs. But that's not really the case. Is manufacturing scrap really necessary, and a sales commission really discretionary? Cost control needs to be maintained in all areas of the business, because a higher price cannot fully recover the impact of a higher cost, as discussed in 3.4. You need to characterize costs in much greater detail to fully understand your business situation, and take steps for improvement. How often should you do this? All the time. Scrutiny and improvement need to be continuous.

Below is a breakdown of marketing costs for a product line of a division of an international corporation. This marketing organization is responsible for marketing activities such as new product research, existing product advertising, and also for the sales function. The sales function, in this organization, goes beyond the taking of an order. A full range of customer relationships, such as warranty repair cost, are included. Clearly, warranty repair cost is a matter of product quality determined by the design and manufacturing functions. Marketing, doesn't directly control this. Yet it's shown as a marketing expense here. Other items, such as allocation to pay for a corporate marketing staff, are also not directly under division marketing control. To fully understand what's happening, the marketing manager needs to know the source of the cost, who controls the cost, whether it's product related (ideally variable or fixed), where in the accounting ledgers it can be found, how large is one cost item compared to another, etc.

Function	Basis	Product/ sales related (P)
Corporate sales people pay	% time reported	P
Service center support to sales	U.S. order forecast	–
Demonstrator repair	actual cost report	P
Customer accommodations	as reported	P
Product support specialist pay	100% of cost	P
Export distributor commission	13% of export sales	P
Field office staff allocation	% of U.S. order forecast	–
Corporate marketing staff allocation	% of U.S. order forecast	–
Division marketing product promotion	actual as budgeted	P
Corporate PR allocation	% division promotion budget	–
Corporate marketing. training allocation	% U.S. orders forecast	–
Corporate marketing export support allocation	% U.S. orders forecast	–
Corporate product distribution allocation	% net world sales forecast	–
Corporate distributor sales allocation	% distributor. orders forecast	–
Instrument warranty repairs	as reported	P
Service center overhead allocation	% U.S. order forecast	–
Corporate marketing assets depreciation	% U.S order forecast	–

The above is a formidable list, and it deals only with marketing. The total picture is even more complicated. But you need this level of detail if you want to know what's happening to you, let alone have some control of the results.

The above lists a large number of charges which depend on an order forecast. Charges are fixed regardless of actual sales once a forecast is established. That's why these items are identified as not product sales dependent. Such an arrangement puts a high premium on meeting sales targets. A shortfall in sales is bad enough in its own right, leading to a deficiency in expected revenue and profit. Here, the result is exacerbated as fixed cost allocations eat up the little bit of profit that's left.

The opposite is also true. Exceed the sales forecast and profit will increase beyond normal levels because much of the cost is fixed. This situation can create all sorts of unpleasant politics as divisions try to get away with the lowest possible order forecasts. But that may not be a good reason not to do it this way. A corporate climate where targets are set in a very conservative manner will eliminate much of the negotiation turmoil. Once set, division management has a very strong incentive to meet order targets. And this is exactly what corporate management may want to achieve.

- **Expense analysis.** Adding the numbers in the above list (individual numbers not given) shows that less than 20% is under direct divisional control. Most of this is in the promotional budget, which is difficult to do without if the order plan is to be met. The marketing staff costs only 9% of the total. Like the federal budget, mandated expenses totally overwhelm discretionary items. There's very little divisional control of marketing costs here. Orders, orders, orders has to be the emphasis in the marketing arena. On the other hand, a similar analysis for manufacturing will show that cost, cost, cost has to be the emphasis there.

6.11 Transfer discount, impact on earnings

Suppose your foreign sales subsidiary offers a significant increase in orders if you would just increase the transfer price discount by 10%. Should you do it? The answer depends on what end result you want to emphasize, and whether the additional discount will yield that result. Suppose your need is to emphasize earnings as a percent of net sales. Then an analysis of the income statement (IS) for the business will help provide an answer.

We begin with an analysis of the IS on the basis of fixed and variable (sales level) related costs. There are two ways to do it. One way uses a projection of historical information, and the other involves a detailed cost analysis along the lines discussed in 6.10. Ideally, you do both, and try to reconcile any differences.

To use historical data, you need to find a number of relatively recent months where sales and earnings differ from month to month. Make sure that there's no significant distortion due to mis-timing of some major revenue and associated cost items. A graphical or direct mathematical analysis will yield the numbers for the relationship between: net sales (NS), variable manufacturing cost of sales (VCOS), other variable costs that change directly with sales (OVC), fixed cost (FC), and income before tax (IBT). Thus: (NS) (1 – VCOS% – OVC%) – FC = IBT.

For example. With a VCOS of 30%. One accounting period shows net sales of $3 million and IBT = $390,000 (13%), another period sales were $4 million and IBT at 20%, etc. A best fit to the data yields OVC = 30% and FC = $800,000.

Now consider the impact of transfer price discounts. Suppose international sales accounts for 25% of total. Then whatever discount (D) is provided will affect VCOS for the business in accordance with the relationship VCOS (new) = (100 VCOS) / (100 – 0.25D). We've assumed here that the 25% ratio remains unchanged with changing discount level to simplify the problem.

From the above formula, we find that an increase in transfer price discount by 10% will increase the total business variable cost of sales by 1.026 times. Hence the original VCOS of 30% becomes a VCOS of 30.8%. We have lost 0.8% of net sales, and the same on the bottom line. Unless, of course, the international sales level is sufficiently increased to offset the loss in earnings. Suppose the normal net sales level is $4 million, with $3 million domestic and one international (25%), and IBT = $800,000 (20%). Now VCOS = 30.8%, OVC is still 30% and FC = $800,000. Total sales need to increase to $4.165 million in order to maintain 20% earnings on sales. Thus:

4,165 (1 – 0.308 – 0.30) – 800 = 832.7

832.7 / 4,165 = 0.20

Now we have a basis for making a decision on the request for a greater transfer price discount. The sales level needs to increase from $1 million, per whatever accounting period was used for this analysis, to 1.165 million. Naturally, the analysis has all sorts of deficiencies, and various adjustments could be attempted. The export sales ratio will be more than the 25% used in the calculation. Manufacturing cost might go down because of greater volume. You might need more people or machinery to increase output, etc. Personally, I wouldn't bother with these items, as the original formulas are pretty sloppy to start with. The point is that we now have a much better feel for what needs to happen to export sales.

6.12 Turns ratios

I vaguely remember, from many years ago, a charge of high prices at a grocery store. The store claimed that prices were very reasonable as their profit was only 1.5%. I remember wondering how it was possible for them to stay in business with such a low profit. After all, a simple bank book offered a much better rate of return on invested money. My confusion was based on two errors. One factor is that you can't compare return numbers unless these refer to the same base measure. Return on sales is not the same as return on invested capital. My second error was to ignore the time period associated with the numbers. Bank interest for one quarter is not the same as interest for one year, for example. The store was selling and replenishing all of their inventory, on the average, ten times per year. The same investment was used (turned) over and over again ten times per year. Their return on investment was 1.5% every tenth of a year, and 15% for a full year. It's the 15% return that we should compare to a bank deposit and not the 1.5%.

Return on sales must be positive, or else you're losing money. The number itself, though, can be misleading. If you can invest $100 to purchase some items which you deliver to someone's home at a charge of $101 (assume you walk and no expenses), and you do this ten times a day for 200 days in the year, then your profit for the year will be $2,000. That's certainly a much more impressive result than the 1% return per transaction. To see the full picture, you need to multiply the return on sales by the turns ratio of whatever measurement base you want to consider. The base most often used is invested capital, and the measurement is known as return on invested capital, ROIC. ROIC is computed as the product of percent return on sales and the turns ratio of invested capital.

For a corporate entity, there's some small difference between capital and assets, involving debt accounts. Otherwise, the two are the same. Return on assets is given by:

ROA = (% profit) (asset turns)

ROA = (earnings / sales) (sales / assets) = earnings / assets

Total asset turns is the result of the turns on various asset types, such as cash, receivables, or work in process. These turn ratios are indicators of business health, and important control tools for management. For example, if an organization generates 100% of sales at a manufacturing cost of sales of 42% and other total costs of 46%, the percent profit margin is 100 − 42 − 46 = 12%. If cash turns 40X per year, receivables turn 8X, inventory turns 6X, fixed assets turn 5X and other remaining assets turn at 20X. Then, the total asset turn ratio is 1.76X from:

1 / 40 + 1 / 8 + 1 / 6 + 1 / 5 + 1 / 20 = 1 / 1.76

ROA = (12) (1.76) = 21%.

Suppose we expect a business expansion and we build a new factory, but orders don't materialize so that fixed assets now turn only at 4X. Suppose further that the same business contraction causes our customers to pay more slowly so that receivables now turn at only 6X. Furthermore, we've built up our inventory stock which isn't selling well and inventory turns are reduced to 5X. Then total assets turn at 1.45 times, and ROA is reduced from 21% to 17.4%, even if return on sales remains unchanged.

Here's a different example. We invest in machinery which significantly improves the build cycle, so that products can be built to order. The new machinery degrades fixed asset turns from 5X to 4X, but inventory turns improve from 6X to 10X. Then, total assets turn at 1.82 times and ROA = 21.8%, even if there's no boost in sales due to better delivery time.

6.13 Low volume products

In every business, there's a certain units volume below which sales become unprofitable. In a business where a normal run rate is at about

1,000, it's common to take 100 as the "low runner" cut off. However, this doesn't always work for very expensive or very profitable products. Furthermore, 100 units is just a guess based on the fact that we use a decimal system. Why not 90 or 110 units? We need a more rigorous decision process based on contribution to profit.

Two measures of profit need to be considered here. One is the standard income statement bottom line measure (I prefer before tax), IBT. The other measure looks at contribution towards fixed costs. In other words, income before fixed cost, IBFC. Both measures need to be used, as shown below.

The crossover between making a contribution and not making a contribution, in accordance with these measures, is the crossover between a financially contributing product and one that reduces overall business profit. Contribution criteria are as follows:

- A positive IBT represents profit and a negative IBT represents loss. The crossover point is at zero IBT.

- One might take that zero is also the crossover point for IBFC. But that isn't the case because every organization has guidelines respecting cash flow and cost of money. You need to recover, as minimum, the cost of capital involved in the cash use to build the product. I chose an IBFC floor of 10% based on my experience of a 50%[6] of sales cash use and a 20% cost of money (an easy to use number, but somewhat high as I write this in 1994). The procedure doesn't depend on the exact number, and the reader can use whatever numbers fit an individual circumstance.

From the above we have two criteria:

---

[6] The 50% number is based on a variable cost of about 50% of sales. This is approximately the working capital needed to maintain these products for sale. There's no offsetting positive cash flow since these products provide hardly any profit. Clearly, this is a very crude approximation that ignores many factors such as the cost of inventory, for example. Furthermore, this is not a new use of cash. The working capital needs to be invested only once. No new investment is needed unless the sale and manufacturing level is increased. The reader may consider that a different number is more appropriate, and that's fine. Whatever number you use, though, should have an understood basis.

- A product which contributes positive IBC is not a low runner.

- A product that has negative IBT and less than 10% IBFC is a low runner.

A product that has negative IBT and more than 10% IBFC needs to be converted to one of the above cases. The conversion involves adding IBFC above 10% to the negative IBT. If the result is positive then we do not have a low runner. If the result is still negative, then we do have a low runner.

Here's an example of the conversion process.

Product	Orders (1,000$)	IBT (1,000$)	IBFC
A	529	–183	48.2%
B	435	–200	47.6%
C	545	–193	51.9%

Combining the measures:

A	529 (0.482-0.1) – 183 = +$19	Not low runner
B	435 (0.476 – 0.1) – 200 = –$36	Low runner
C	545 (0.519 – 0.1) – 193 = +$35	Not low runner

A decision about discontinuing the sale of these products needs to involve more than financial considerations. A low runner may make a strategic contribution to a product group and have to be retained for the sake of other products. Conversely, a product just out of low runner territory might be removed because it has no strategic importance, and gets in the way of more important concerns. Therefore, a decision should not be based solely on a financial computation. Such a computation will, however, help pick products for further analysis.

6.14 Manufacturing relationships

Manufacturing is a major discipline in its own right. This isn't a book, or a chapter, or even a section that explains "manufacturing". The objective here is to deal with one specific issue that affects profitability and, hence, pricing.

People sometimes confuse orders with sales. An order is booked when someone provides a request, usually by a document called a purchase order, for delivery of a product that you offer for sale. You have a sale when the product is delivered and the customer is asked for payment via an invoice. Sometimes, the sale is not recorded until you're paid, because the shipment is contingent on customer testing and acceptance of the goods. Orders can be, and are sometimes, cancelled. A cancelled order will not turn into a sale. An order is the egg which turns into a sale when the egg becomes a chicken.

An order places a demand upon manufacturing to output, that is build, the product for shipment to the customer. Orders-on-hand is called unfilled demand. Demand that is filled becomes sales. Demand can be filled from current manufacturing output or from finished goods inventory previously built by manufacturing. Thus, we need to balance several items. These are:

D = demand, i.e. incoming orders.

UD = unfilled demand, orders previously received but not yet filled.

S = sales, i.e. shipments to customers to fulfill demand.

O = production output which turns either into sales or finished goods inventory.

FGI = finished goods inventory previously built which can be used to fulfill orders demand.

For any time period, FGI and UD have a starting point, s, and an ending point, e.

The difference between the starting and ending quantities is the change (CH) in these items. Thus:

$(CH)\ UD = UD_s - UD_e$.

$FGI_s + O = TAG$ the total available goods for sale.

$TAG - S = FGI_e$ remaining finished goods.

$UD_s + D = TD$ the total demand.

$TD - S = UD_e$ remaining demand.

FGIs + O – S = FGIe

UDs + D – S = UDe

Adding the two equations and adjusting terms, yields:

FGIs – FGIe + UDs – UDe + O + D = 2S

But:

FGIs – FGIe = (CH) FGI

UDs – UDe= (CH) UD

Hence:

S = (1/2) (CH) FGI + (CH) UD + O + D.

(1) FGIs – UDs = finished goods not covered by demand at start.

(2) FGIe – UDe = finished goods not covered by demand at the end.

(1) – (2) = change in finished goods not covered by demand.

(3) O – D = change in finished goods not covered by demand.

(1) – (2) = (3) (CH) FGI + D = (CH) UD + O

Hence:

S = (1/2) (CH) FGI + (CH) UD + O + D

S = (CH) FGI + D

S = (CH) UD + O

A change in manufacturing output rate (O) affects working capital. An increase in manufacturing output represents a negative cash flow which is stored in the finished goods inventory. We'll eventually recover this cost when the product is discontinued. In the meantime, we've made an investment in our business. The negative cash use is offset by a positive flow to the extent that the sale provides profits. For analysis purposes I've taken cash use to be at 50% of sales based on roughly 50% cost of goods sold.

The above relationships permit a comparison among various strategic choices, such as more sales and profits now, versus a greater unfilled demand cushion to protect against a business decline later.

Consider the following example. At the end of the fiscal year (same as beginning position for next year), we have:

UD = $14 (million or whatever)

FGI = $3.0

O = $21.0 (during just finished year)

D = $33.0 (forecasted for next year)

Suppose we want to get the very highest possible level of cash flow. This means that we want to minimize manufacturing output while getting as much cash from sales as we can. Hence, we want to ship all of our finished goods inventory, and FGI will go to zero (not possible realistically, but we are playing "what if" here).

$$S = (CH)\ FGI + D = (CH)\ UD + O$$

Letting FGI go to zero means that $S = 3 + D = (CH)\ UD + O$. We now need to choose an unfilled demand. We want delivery time not to exceed 13 weeks, or one quarter of a year. Hence:

$$UD = D / 4$$

$$S = 3 + D = 14 - D/4 + O$$

Cash use to build more products is:

$$CU = (1/2)\ (Pe - Ps) = (1/2)\ (O - 21)$$

$$O = 2CU + 21$$

$$S = 3 + D = 14 - 0.25D + 2CU + 21$$

For every value of demand, D, we get corresponding values of sales, S, and cash use, CU. If the forecast is met at D = 33. Then, S = 36, and CU = 4.6. If the order forecast has an uncertainty range of, say $27 to $35 million, we can find sales and cash need numbers for the whole range. The result can be plotted on a graph to show a dynamic relationship between demand, sales, cash use, etc.

Near $5 million in cash use doesn't look very attractive. But this isn't the complete picture because we also have a positive cash flow from profits. Here, we need to look at a model of the income statement. A 7% profit margin on $36 million in sales will cut total cash need by $2.5 million, for example.

It should be noted that effective use of these, or other such relationships, is more complicated than it might appear. For example, a high unfilled demand may look attractive as a hedge against an uncertain future but it also indicates a long delivery time. Customers may not be willing to wait, and orders will suffer. Choice of a relatively short delivery cycle, such as 13 weeks, seems reasonable until we examine the composition of the $14 million backlog. Why didn't we ship these orders last year? Perhaps we have some large yearly orders that need to be delivered at specified intervals. An average delivery time of 13 weeks will not work here. It's also necessary to take care in using definitions for quantities. Orders, for example, are usually booked at gross prices while sales are recorded as a net value after discount.

A quote from Tucker – *Handbook of Business Formulas and Controls* – McGraw-Hill, expresses my sentiments precisely. This book is full of formulas, sometimes ten on one page. Yet, Dr. Tucker says that "problem solving abounds with procedures and rituals resembling primitive tribal rites. The activity resembles the practice of sorcery and witchcraft, where the witch doctor dances around the tribal fire and divines magic numbers from which decisions are made." Never forget that a formula is not a substitute for thinking.

6.15 International distribution pricing

The relationship between the parent organization and product distributor or sales organizations will have an important impact on sales levels, profits, and prices. Every situation is different. Hence what follows is intended only as an example of process rather than a specific formula for success for all cases. The case involves a US based company that sells its products outside the US through independent sales organizations. The issue at hand is how to set the price for best balance between profit and market share.

- The past choice in international, whether deliberate or not, has been to sacrifice growth in favor of profit. Here's the basis for that conclusion.

International product orders increased by 15.7% CAGR in the last four years. This represents 3.7% growth per year. The best estimate of market growth during this time is between 8% and 10% per year. This represents a market share change ratio to 0.85, assuming the 8% market growth figure. Current market share is only 0.85 of what it was four years ago.

The organization has introduced several new products during this period. Orders in the US grew by 66%, or 13.5% per year, during the same years. We gained share in the US.

The contribution to profit of the sales subsidiaries has held steady (maybe a slight increase) during the same time frame.

- The consensus conclusion is that we lost international share because of the following:

   - The competition has become much more aggressive in these geographies.

   - Our market segments have become more price sensitive.

   - Our philosophy has been to price for profit.

- A profit analysis:

Price details for an international sale are more complicated than for a domestic sale, as follows:

Q = 100% of current units level

P = end customer selling price at $ equivalent

TR = transfer price from US parent to selling organization

VC = variable product selling cost, such as import duty

F = selling organization operating cost, taken as an allocated fixed constant

E = selling organization earnings, or profit

Then:

$$E = Q (P - TR - VC) - F$$

- A P-V analysis.

The current situation is as follows: Q = 100%. The international selling price is P = 120% of the US domestic selling price. The transfer discount is at 20% of the US price, and TR = 80%. The variable selling cost is VC = 10%, and the (assumed) fixed cost is F = 23%. The result is that E = 7%.

The market is known to be price sensitive and elastic. Unit volume changes more than price. A max/min estimate is that unit volume changes at between two and three times the price change.

For a price reduction of P = 110 vs 120 now. Q = 120 vs 100 now.

E = 1% vs 7% now. The other P-V estimate is that a change to P =110 yields Q = 130 and E = 3%, which is 3.9% on an absolute revenue basis versus 7% now.

A price increase to P = 130 results in Q = 80 and E = 9%, which is the same as the current 7% on an absolute basis. The other P-V estimate shows that for P = 130, Q = 70 and E = 5%, or 3.5% on an absolute basis.

Clearly, profit for the selling organization is better at the current, or even a higher, price. But that's not the whole story. We are slowly losing market share and going out of business. Furthermore, manufacturing is operating well below capacity at a fixed cost of almost 30% of current output. International sales take half the output. A 20% increase in international orders will increase manufacturing demand by 10%, and reduce costs by over 2%. In addition, the current factory-based margin on export sales is near 8%. This makes for a total of 15% when we include the sales organization.

- Strategic balance.

Profit optimization pricing for the selling organization is adversely affecting the strategic market position for the total business. Total margin, including capacity utilization changes and margin on sales for the home office, will improve with higher volume and offset the impact on the selling organization of a price reduction. Currently the home office sets the transfer price (TR) to achieve its margin objectives, and the selling organization sets its selling price (P) to achieve its margin objectives. This doesn't optimize overall results. The business can, so to speak, have the cake and eat it too, provided pricing is done on an integrated basis. A reduction in transfer price that is matched by at least an equal reduction in end-user selling price will increase market share without an adverse impact on total business profit margin.

6.16 Measures of profit

Profit is what's left after you pay your expenses. That's true. But that doesn't mean that this is the only, or even the best, measure of profitability or business health. A low return on sales may not be a poor profit at all if you have a high turns ratio (see 6.12). Certainly, you need a positive residue of earnings in order to claim a profit. But there are many ways to look at the result after that.

• There's a difference between economic and accounting income. The economist compares the value of assets at the end of the accounting period to the value at the beginning, and that's your income. The total involves income from operations, such as the sale of a product, and the changed valuation of assets, such as stock owned by the company. The accountant, however, differentiates between realized and unrealized income. The appreciation of the stock will not be counted until you sell the stock and can spend the proceeds.

• But the accountant does count, so called, realized income even when it is not yet available because of accrual accounting. Only a cash system will truly show actual income available for immediate use.

• Profit is usually taken to be the bottom line of the income statement, called **earnings** by accountants and **income** by people like me. Income is an absolute monetary amount, such as $1,000. You have income before tax (IBT), and income after tax (IAT). Naturally, the final remaining profit is what remains after you pay taxes. Corporate financial management devise various strategies aimed at reducing the tax load. This, however, is well beyond the expertise of this author or the intent of this book. I believe that it's best to use measures that one can, at least to some degree, influence. Hence, my preference for IBT for all but the treasury function or highest levels of corporate management.

- An income of $1,000 is not much to live on. But it's an indicator of good business efficiency if the sum was earned on $5,000 in revenue. An **income percentage of revenue** of $1 / 5 = 20\%$ is a good operating return.

- Sometimes the percent income looks very poor, say 1%. But the time frame in which it is earned is small, say one month. For the year then, the return will be 12%, and that's good. We need to look at the time frame, or **turns**, associated with a percentage result to determine what it really means. Any use of capital has a turns ratio associated with it (see 6.12).

- Profit is not the same as cash in the bank with which to pay your bills. Particularly heavy use of cash occurs when starting a new business or new project, as you pay for buildings and equipment and salary to the people who are developing the business. Such a business not only has negative cash flow, but also negative profits, until there's income from sales. Another example involving negative **cash flow** is a very fast growing business with good sales and good profits. Growth, involves use of cash to support a growing infrastructure and work in process inventory.

Cash flow analysis is fairly simple for a basic entity, like an operating business unit. The primary source of cash is earnings on sales and cash use goes into assets like machinery and inventory. A corporation will frequently establish cash flow guidelines for individual operating units, like divisions. Those whose mandate is to grow, will be net cash users. Another, sometimes called a "cash cow", is required to be a net cash supplier. For a corporation as a whole, a cash source and use statement, or a cash flow statement, will be much more complicated. Thus, sources of cash will involve: retained earnings, reduction of cash on-hand, increase in debt, increase in accounts payable (we pay our bills more slowly, so have more cash), etc. Uses of cash will include:

increase in inventory, increase in plant and equipment, increase in accounts receivable (our customers are paying us more slowly), etc.

Why should we care about cash flow? Because we have to pay our bills. If necessary, we will have to borrow money. This reduces the profit because we have to repay the loan with interest.

- The **payback, payoff,** or **payout** period is a measure of how long it will take to recover the cost of an initial investment. Suppose we invest $16,000 in a machine that will provide $4,000 per year in operating cost savings. The payback period is 16 / 4 = 4 years. Another proposal involves a $12,000 machine that will also yield $4,000 of yearly savings. Clearly, this looks like a better deal because the payback period is shorter. But a shorter payback may not represent the best business decision. After all, you can have an instantaneous payback if you do not make the investment in the first place. Suppose the $16,000 machine will last 10 years while the $12,000 one only 3 years. There's no residual return from this investment at all, because the machine becomes useless just as its cost is recovered after 3 years. The user needs to take care that payback comparisons take into account all the variables.

- The **accounting rate-of-return** attempts to correct some of the payback procedure shortcomings by including useful life information by means of depreciation. Depreciation for a $16,000 item that lasts 10 years is $1,600 per year. The accounting rate of return is calculated at (4,000 − 1,600) / 16,000 = 15%. An alternate procedure uses the average life of the asset, which is half the original when using equal yearly depreciation and zero value at end of life. The result for our calculation is then 30%.

- Neither the payback period nor the accounting rate-of-return tell the whole story because these ignore the time-value of money. The initial investment is made the first year, but the payback occurs over several subsequent years. The current value of the income you receive in future years is less than, it's depreciated from, the amount you will receive. Depreciated calculation of cash flow, earnings, investments or whatever aims at making a fair comparison by taking time-value costs into consideration. The result is called the **net present value.** The choice of the depreciation rate to use depends on what you want to emphasize — inflation, cost of borrowing, current corporate return on capital, etc. Names associated with the depreciation used are indicative of the various choices — required rate, hurdle rate, cutoff rate, discount rate, target rate, cost of capital rate, etc.

Whatever the discount rate, the calculation is fairly simple. The value of one monetary unit received in the future is discounted at the appropriate rate per year until it's brought into the present. Thus, at a rate of 8% we have: 1 / 1.08 = 0.926 after one year, 0.926 / 1.08 = 0.857 after two years, etc. Virtually all books on finance have present value tables, so you just look up the results. Thus, if we invest $1,000 today and this yields various income levels in future years, the net present value using an 8% discount rate is computed as:

Year	0	1	2	3	4	5	6
income	−1,000	400	300	300	200	100	0
NPV @ 8%	1.0	0.926	0.857	0.794	0.735	0.681	
NPV	−1,000	370.4	257.1	238.2	147.0	68.1	

Ordinary cash flow shows a $1,300 return on the $1,000 investment, but the discounted result is only $1,080.7.

Note that discounted calculations involve a time component. Great care must be exercised to ensure that timing is correctly treated. Accrual accounting ledgers cannot be used here.

- The **internal rate of return** is a corollary to the net present value problem. Here we determine the discount rate that will yield a net present value of zero. This is then compared to the hurdle rate to determine a figure of merit for the project. Hand calculation of an internal rate of return is rather tricky and involves a trial and error procedure. However, no one need do it manually. Most financial function calculators will do it for you.

For example, a current investment of $3,038, that yields $1,000 per year for 4 years, has an internal rate of return of 12%. The NPV of $1,000 at 12% for 4 years, provides: 893 + 797 + 712 + 636 = 3,038.

- A procedure, or transaction, either external or internal to your organization will usually provide a measurable **business result**. An example of an external transaction would be a sale to a customer or a purchase from a supplier. A change in pay policy would be an example of an internal operation that affects business results. There are, literally, hundreds of possible measures of internal and external procedures and transactions and their ratios. Any book on business finance will explain the most useful or popular. What's useful depends on the point of view, or relationship to the business, of the user. Business managers care about profit and profit margin as a percent of sales, various turn ratios such as total assets or work in process or receivables, and so on. The stockholder owners, on the other hand, are interested in such things as net worth, or equity or earnings per share of stock. The banker who lends you money wants to know about your ability to service the debt. Cash flow, ratio of assets to liabilities, and other related ratios will be of interest here. There are also other interested parties. Employees are usually interested in sales and people growth, as this is an indicator of job security and possibility of promotion. Government agencies want to make sure you operate in a legal manner and pay your taxes. Your local community will have an interest in your investment in pollution control assets. And so on. These are connected by a complicated web of behavior and happenings, mostly not under the direct control of the business manager. There is, however, one decision which is, at least in theory, completely under your control — the decision to choose a price.

- **Price**, by itself, is not a business result or health of business indicator. It is, however, a critical driver of results, and it's essentially under your direct control. Market share depends on sales revenue, and sales revenue is connected to price through the demand relationship. The need to increase work-in-process inventory is determined by the order rate, which in turn is affected by price. Price times quantity orders establishes revenue income. Less expenses and you have profit. There is no profit without a sale, and there's no sale without a price. You can set a strategic target for earnings, for sales level, for assets employed, for anything. But these are not under your direct control. That's why we call these strategic targets. The price, however, is under your control. You can choose any price you want, at least in theory. Sure, there are factors that push you towards one or another price level. Customer perceived value, competitor behavior, costs, are price drivers. You would not be doing your job if you didn't pay attention to these. But in theory, you could choose any price you like, even if it lost you your business. Price is the only direct variable that you can completely control. Furthermore, it's a factor that, either directly or indirectly, affects the other factors. You can't, for example, directly make the sales level be some particular value. You must do it indirectly through advertising, product feature differentiation, or price. That's why the theme of this book is that price affects everything.

6.17 Matrix strategies

Portfolio management, life cycle analysis, matrix strategies, and other such procedures approach strategic planning from a global, rather than an individual detail, point of view. Global, or universal, principles are applied to strategic decision making. In most cases the result can be graphed as a two dimensional matrix, representing regions of attractive and unattractive strategic choice. Hence, the general term, matrix strategies. I will provide two abbreviated examples here. The reader will find numerous books and general literature dealing with various aspects of this area.

- The **life cycle** is a well established business phenomenon. Like a living organism, a product, market segment, or technology is born, grows, matures, and dies. To be sure, some live longer than others, and some seem to be around a very long time indeed. But, most products are either completely replaced by something else, or undergo a significant rejuvenation process. Whether it be product, market, technology, or whatever, the strategic importance, and hence management process, differs as a function of life-cycle position.

Full use of the life cycle idea will manage each entity in accordance with its life cycle position and manage the business as a whole for a balanced portfolio of life-cycle positions. New investment slows, and sales growth will slow or decline as a product or market ages. This will generate a positive cash flow which can be used to finance development of a newly emerging market or product. Penetrating a market and getting market share is relatively easy (assuming you have something to sell) in a newly emerging area. There are lots of newly emerging customers who will give you a try. Furthermore, the competition may still be learning how to do it right. Not so for an aging market. Every sale you get will be contested by an entrenched competitor. Are there exceptions? Certainly, there are always exceptions. Come up with a totally new procedure that cuts the price in half and you can do very well even in an old and established market. Usually, though a new competitor will not do well in an older market.

Whether, market, technology or whatever, we talk about four maturity stages: emerging, growing, mature, and aging. Generally, sales increase from zero until the beginning of the aging phase and then start to decline. The converse is true for investment cash use. The investment is heavy in the beginning and we get a positive cash return at the end.

Not only the life cycle stage, but your position in the market place vis-a-vis the competition, will determine your behavior. A weak competitor in an aging market should plan a withdrawal strategy. A strong competitor in a growing market, however, should follow an investment strategy. Similarly, a strong competitor in an aging market may follow a cash flow strategy to finance the growing business segment. But be careful not to "kill the goose that lays the golden eggs" unless the growth product is a replacement for the aging one.

All sorts of business decisions can be considered from a life-cycle point of view. Take technology, for example. The most volatile position is in the emerging stage. This also happens to be one of the most interesting and exciting stages technically. Scientists will promise you the whole universe if you'll just spend an adequate amount on research. That's a perilous road to follow. Business conditions and technical considerations should drive the investment decision, but not the personal excitement of the research scientists.

- **Portfolio management** strategy comes in many flavors. Some of what I discussed in the life cycle section deals with a portfolio matrix with life stage on one axis and company competitive strength on the other.

One of the best known portfolio formulations was publicized by the Boston Consulting Group. Here, the axes are market growth versus relative market share. They use colorful names like "cash cow" for a business in the high share and low market growth quadrant. This could be the aging life stage market I discussed before. Such a situation offers positive cash flow, hence a "cash cow." A high share in a high growth market is a "star" to be invested in for the future, etc.

Portfolio strategies is a tool, like any other. Much useful insight can be obtained from this procedure. But like the rote use of formulas, it shouldn't be relied upon blindly. Just because the model says that something is a "dog" and should be discontinued doesn't mean that you have to do it. Think before you act. Is it profitable? Will customers get angry and take revenge on your other products? How much time or resources will you gain by exiting this business? Can you, and what will it take to get the business into a more favorable position? Etc.

6.18 Limits to growth

The usual big dream is to capture 100% share of a very high growth business segment. And if we can't get 100%, then surely we should manage 50%. But, the world seldom cooperates, and the result is a failure like the one discussed in 4.4. There appear to be certain universal self-limiting mechanisms that limit uncontrolled growth whether it be of epidemics, or market share. Furthermore, the relative size of businesses appears to be in inverse proportion to the rank order of size —1/1, 1/2, 1/3, 1/4, 1/5, etc., in accordance with Zipf's law. Recent studies indicate a "natural" 2:1 market share among direct competitors, unless there's a major structural dislocation, such as a new scientific discovery, or the larger competitor pretty much abandons the business. This says that if the leader has 45% and you are in second place with 15%, you better have some very clever tricks up your sleeve if your objective is to achieve 30%. Indeed, 25% is most unlikely, as this implies either killing some that follow you or gaining close to parity with the leader.

Not only share, but total market size also has growth limitations. Most people have trouble visualizing the exponential growth of compounding. Thus, 15% growth per year will double in size every 5 years. There's an ancient story about the discovery of chess. The king was so delighted that he offered the inventor a room full of jewels. No, said the wise inventor. He just wanted some grain. One kernel on the first square of the board, two on the second square, four on the third, and so on, doubling every square. What a fool, thought the king, until he discovered that there wasn't enough grain in the whole world to fulfill this request. Forever is a long time, and nothing can grow in a geometric progression, even for a relatively short time.

Here's a typical starting point for a strategic plan. There are 5 competitors in the market and you are number two in size. The market share positions are 55%, 20%, 10%, 10%, 5%. The market is growing at 25% / year and you decide to increase your share to 30% in 5 years. This looks like a modest growth of just 30 / 20 = 1.5 times in 5 years. But consider. The size of the market will increase by a factor of 3X at 25% per year for 5 years. Your sales rate will go from a current base level of 20 to 30% of 300, or 90. You will grow by 90 / 20 = 4.5 times in 5 years, and not 1.5 times as you thought. What will the other competitors be doing during this time? Your increase in share will have to come from somewhere, after all. How about the market. Will it continue to grow at 25% for five more years? What will you do with the excess output capacity you plan to build if the market does not grow, or your competitors fight back?

Certainly, an aggressive strategic plan is not all bad. We all know of cases where somebody struck it rich. But just in case, try to protect yourself with a contingency scenario and have some respect for the power of large numbers.

6.19 Contingency plans

I remember a lecture on business strategy in a course that I attended. The professor was discussing success factors. "Now", he said "we come to the most important success factor of all, good luck." Luck, both good and bad strikes everybody sometimes. But the professor was not talking about a random chance event. Certainly that happens, but this is not a treatise on how to win the lottery. What the professor was talking about is the ability to take advantage of good luck. To recognize an opportunity when it comes your way and to be prepared to take advantage of it. Even more important is the recognition of "bad luck" and the ability to overcome it.

Bad luck is very likely because of the law of unintended consequences. Unintended and undesired results are quite frequent when you are engaged in a complex strategy. Even a simple undertaking can bring an unpleasant surprise. Suppose you are driving to work and hear on the radio about a major traffic accident on your main route. You will know which alternate route to take if you know the area, and have done a proper job of contingency planning. It will cost you a bit of extra time, but your day will not be a loss. A newcomer to the area, though, might be stuck in traffic for hours. To be effective, a contingency plan needs to include two essential elements.

- A detailed understanding of the business. The newcomer in the traffic example may have a contingency plan to go around the congested area. But, it will do no good if the person is not familiar with the local street system.

- A danger warning, or monitoring system. You will not avoid the traffic jam if you do not know about it in time to take evasive action.

An additional essential element involves a decision on whether the problem warrants a change in plan (will the traffic be stalled for five minutes or five hours), and which of several contingencies to implement. Here you need to consider where, among three possibilities, the problem resides.

- One possible problem is that the plan or strategy is poorly conceived. You will not achieve the intended objective, even if everything that was planned is perfectly carried out. Spending resources on such a plan can be worse than doing nothing. You need to move, as soon as possible, to a different plan, different actions, and, likely, different objectives as well.

- The plan is an excellent plan but you don't have the resources to carry it out. Either you find the additional resources (extremely difficult to do, so watch out for wishful thinking), or you stop. A high impact plan poorly carried out usually yields much inferior results than a less ambitious plan carried out well.

- The plan is good and the resources are available but some things didn't quite work out as intended. It's very rare, and does indeed require good luck, for all elements of a complicated plan to go exactly as planned. Something will usually go wrong. Here's where persistence pays off. Part of the plan, or a contingency to it, should be a procedure for learning from the problems so it can be done better the second time around. Here, "if at first you don't succeed try, try again" is a good choice. However, if you are faced with an unworkable plan, or as is more likely, a serious lack of resources, then you may have to change to a different plan. The sooner you recognize this the better off you will be. Here you follow the rule that "if at first you don't succeed, redefine success".

6.20 Financial result objectives

Section 5.12 starts with the words: "Do an analysis of contribution-to-profit using whatever relationship fits your business methodology". Section 2.7 states that: "The ideal price will meet your financial pricing objectives." One of the axes of the price gap matrix is price vs objective. Throughout this book it's either stated directly or assumed that the business has an established profit objective which the price needs to support. Nowhere, however, do I explain what such an objective should be or how to set it. Now that I am discussing it, it's in a chapter dealing with supplementary material. Why not place this important topic in a more "important" part of the book? The reason is that there are many differing ideas, philosophies, or theories on this topic. A full treatment would take more than this book. Furthermore, I must admit that I'm on shaky grounds when it comes to "expertise" in this specialized area. I cannot tell you precisely what to do or how to do it. But I can give you some ideas on what to consider:

- Should you have a financial objective(s) for a business or product? Certainly you can run a business without having such objectives. Many businesses operate quite successfully that way. But many businesses also fail rather quickly because of it. It should be clear from the content of this book that you do need to have at least one financial objective if you want to set prices on the basis of some rational reasons. The start of the process is an understanding of your convictions respecting the purpose of the business. You will think differently about financial objectives, and behave differently with respect to pricing if you are in business to generate a cash profit surplus which you will withdraw for personal use versus a desire to grow sales so as to provide jobs. I'm not in a position to tell you what you do or should believe about the core purpose of your business. You do have to decide what these beliefs are, and this will form one input in deciding on financial objectives.

- Besides financial objectives, you also need to look at non-financial pricing objectives. Of course, anything related to price eventually has a financial impact. Initially, though, these factors are not directly financial. Here are examples of what I mean:

We want to price so as to:

- Gain market share.

- Grow the size of the market (segment).

- Be the lowest price supplier.

- Be the price leader.

- Maintain market price stability.

- Establish high performance and quality image.

- Avoid attention from competitors.

- Keep competitors out of market.

- Another way to look at financial objectives is to consider the minimum "profit" needed to stay in business. Profit is in quotes because there are several different possible measures of profit. Which measure, or measures, you choose depends on which theory you accept, and what your business objectives are. If your business priority is to grow at a certain rate, then it's possible to compute a minimum needed return on sales per section 3.24, for example. A variety of profit measures are discussed in section 6.16.

It's generally agreed that a business will not survive on a long-term basis unless the return on invested capital (ROIC) is at least equal to the cost of capital. Some people go further and develop a time-based, amortized, investment ROIC which leads to a product target price as discussed by Scheuble in Harvard Business Review, Nov./Dec., 1964. Indeed, there's a position that "profit" is a misleading concept when the, so-called, profit is used to cover cost of capital.

- In general, whatever measure you choose and whatever number you need to achieve, there are usually several ways to get there. Thus, you can get the same return on assets via many combinations of return on sales and asset turns per figure 7.3. This is dictated by your choice of business strategy and, in turn, also dictates what strategy to use.

- Two other factors to consider are impact of and on other products, and the uncertainty of the future. It's enormously rare that some unforeseen event happens that suddenly doubles your profits. But it's not at all rare that something unforeseen happens that turns your profit into a loss. You can only survive by use of surplus profit stored up from the past. Furthermore, not every product can provide all the return that's asked of it. This means that some products must provide more than the minimum necessary. Consequently, you must be careful not to settle for just the minimum needed because over several products, and for some reasonable time period, you will end up with less than is needed.

- Sometimes you have an opportunity to generate not only greater than needed, but also greater than apparently reasonable profit. The need for greater than "needed" profit was explained in the previous bullet. But what about greater than reasonable? Is it good business or honorable to take a greater than reasonable profit? The answer is yes, because there is no unreasonable profit. A transaction may be illegal or unfair, but the concept of unreasonable does not apply here. Usually, a business is used to operating on a certain margin, say 15% of sales, or on a certain multiple of variable cost such as 2.5 times. A return of 40% on sales or a 5X multiple on costs will then seem unreasonable. But these perceptions compare profit against your own internal measures. This is the wrong way to look at it. What counts is whether you are providing value to the customer. The customer will not buy the product even at a profit of 5%, let alone 15% on sales, if the value is not there. Similarly, the customer will be happy to give you a 40% return if the value is there. You can't get an unreasonable profit because the customer will not purchase if the price is unreasonable with respect to value. Your concern should not be whether a 5X multiple on costs is reasonable, should you be in the fortunate position to charge that. Your concern should be for the best business strategy that takes advantage of this opportunity. Suppose, for example, you have a highly desirable new product. People are standing in line to pay a very high price for it. What should you do?

1. You could charge all that the market will accept within the limits of your manufacturing capacity to meet the quantity demand of the P-V curve. You could slowly reduce price over time to track your increased output capability. Similarly, you could drop the price as needed when a competing product becomes available. In the meantime you will be using the "unreasonable" profits to build more factories and to store up a reserve against the day when your profit is reduced below that needed as competitive products get into the market. Viewed this way, the unreasonable profit is not unreasonable, it is in fact needed for the future.

2. You could decide on an experience curve strategy and go for volume. Here you must build more output capacity right away. This means money from other sources. Presumably these other sources involve more than needed profit from other products. Your return on sales will no longer be "unreasonable", but your profit as a return on investment could be just as good, or better than for the high price case. It all depends on the elasticity of the P-V curve. Possibly you will want to do this even if your return on investment is worse than for the high-priced case because it will keep your competitors out of the market and give you a more secure future.

- Eventually you need to translate your profit objective into a price. Remember that the price affects profit in more than one way. Price affects volume, it affects revenue and it affects cash flow. This means that you need to understand P-V results and customer value and behavior for the chosen market segment. Ultimately it's the price times quantity, compared to operating cost and investment level that determines profit or return on investment.

Chapter 7
Appendix

This section provides graphs, tables, and other reference material that you will find useful as you work on your pricing issues. The copyright owner grants the owner of this book permission to photocopy any material from this appendix for their own use.

Much of this material is taken directly from the body of the book — some is a modified version of book material and some items are new. In any event, the appendix is not an abridged version of the book. Much that the reader will need is not replicated here. Therefore, I recommend that you not rely on the appendix as a shortcut to learning what the book contains. First, you need to read and become familiar with the book proper; then, you can use the appendix as an aid when you work on your pricing issues.

7.1 Questions

You know by now that I like to follow a question and answer format. On the next page is a repetition of the analysis questions from section 5.2. See 5.2 for an explanation of what these questions are about. For example. Question 2 — Identify the customer — doesn't ask for the name of a person, but rather identification of a user class or market segment. These questions are followed by other questions and suggestions to help you get the job done. However, you ultimately need to deal with the full range of questions found throughout this book if you want to do a thorough job.

Basic analysis questions

1. Identify the product(s).

2. Identify the customer.

3. Identify critical customer issues related to the product.

4. List major competing products.

5. How well does your product fit the customer's needs (per 3)? Is your product fit to customer value: G (good), M (medium), P (poor)?

6. Do G, M, P designation (#5) for the top 4 competing products.

7. Explain basis for your answers in #5 and #6.

8. Rank order five products from #5 and #6 in accordance with meeting customer needs/value.

9. Explain why your product has the rank position you gave it in #8.

10. Go back to #4 and rank order for customer value. Compare to products in #8.

11. Explain any difference between #10 and #8. Do you want to change anything (choice of competing products or ranking)?

12. List price and value ranking from 11 for your own and competing products.

Product _____ _____ _____ _____ _____

Price _____ _____ _____ _____ _____

Value _____ _____ _____ _____ _____

13. Construct a price-value comparison graph.

V
A
L
U
E

PRICE

14. How does your product compare to competition in #13?

14A. For value — Why are you there? Is that where you want to be? Where would you like to be?

14B. For price — Why are you there? Is that where you want to be? Where would you like to be?

14C. Compare your price/value ratio to competition. Are you in the quadrant you want to be in (e.g., upper right at high value and high price)? Do you want to be someplace else on the chart? What is stopping you?

15. What are your profit objectives?

16. Has your profit objective(s) affected the price? How?

17. Is there a disparity between price based on your profit need, and price based on customer value need?

18. List action items.

Supplementary analysis questions.

1. Describe the environment in which you do business.

   Company philosophy (growth, image, profit, etc.)

   Distribution channels (stores, agents, own sales, etc.)

   External (inflation, legal/regulation, social, etc.)

   Customers (who — users, buyers, specifiers, needs/wants).

   Technology (life cycle position, rate of change, etc.).

2. Describe pricing procedures in your company and in your organization. Are you required to price for a certain margin or multiple of costs? Is there a price adjustment trigger? What is the trigger? Who sets prices? Who approves prices? Is there an established procedure to set or justify a price? Describe procedure?

3. Describe the company and/or organization cost structure. What sort of cost accounting do you use (e.g, fully allocated absorption). What are cost drivers (manufacturing, distribution, technology, etc.)? Fixed vs variable product related costs. Capacity utilization. Use of assets. Etc.

4. Rank order the three top results you want to get as a result of the price. E.g. sales volume, % return on sales, ROIC. Does your current price give this to you? If not, what is stopping you? List action items aimed at getting you closer to your objectives.

7.2 Pricing sequence

This material comes from section 3.1.

The basic pricing sequence consists of the following:

- What is the value?
- What are the objectives?
- What is the profit?
- Is there a gap?
- Fix the gap.

A complete pricing sequence will include additional items, such as:

- Price-demand information.

- Market segments.

- Manufacturing capacity utilization.

- The experience curve.

- Relationship to other products.

- Impact on the future.

- New product pricing.

- Pricing in inflationary times.

- Incremental sales.

- Pricing for market stability.

- Defensive and offensive pricing.

- Bidding.

- Market growth or zero sum?

- Commodity or differentiated product pricing.

- Costing — absorbed or not?

7.3 Price and value comparison

You constructed a price and value comparison graph in section 7.1. The price by itself or the value by itself can be important. A price-sensitive market may not accept a high-priced product even when perceived value is high. Similarly, a performance-oriented market may not accept a low-value product even when the price is low. Usually, however, it's the ratio of perceived value to price that determines how customers will treat you.

From the results of question 13 in section 7.1, how does your V/P ratio compare to the competition? You could be equal, or you are higher or lower. Higher is good, lower not good.

1. Are you happy with the result?

2. Why do you have this result?

3. Do you think that customer perception of value is accurate? If not, then what should it be? What will/can you do about it (advertising, free samples, sales training, etc.)?.

4. What will/can you do about an accurate but unfavorable perception (change product, change price, etc.)?

Place your product on a price gap matrix. Do you want to stay where you are or change? Make a list of possible action items that will result in a favorable change.

7.4 The price gap matrix

See various sections in chapter 2 for more details.

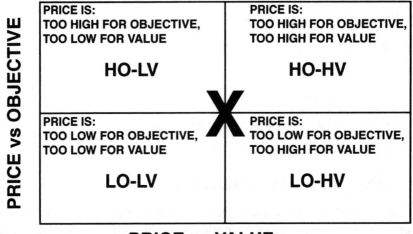

- **HO-LV:** Great place to be if you know what to do with it.

- **LO-LV:** Fairly easy to fix with a price increase. But analyze first for unintended consequences.

- **HO-HV:** Theoretically easy to fix with a price reduction. But analyze first for unintended consequences.

- **LO-HV:** You're in trouble. Reduce costs, improve perceived product value, or get out of this business.

Answers to the following questions will help you decide what to do.

- Why are you where you are and how did you get there?

- Do you want to be where you are, and do you want to or need to move?

- Where do you want to or need to be?

- What do you need to do and what can you actually do to move to the desired location?

7.5 Segments

Pricing strategy must take into account market segments. A market segment consists of a group of customers that have similar ideas about needs, value, ability to pay, etc. You need to separate the total market into semi-autonomous, semi-homogeneous segments. This is an iterative process. You fit the product(s) to the segment(s) and you fit the segment(s) to the product(s). You may choose to develop a new product to address a known segment, or you may try to find a segment that will be interested in an existing product. Either way, there needs to be a fit between segment and product or you will have difficulties.

You have essentially two primary variables along which to segment the market: On the basis of products offered and/or on the basis of customer attributes. Thus, you might segment computers on the basis of speed, or memory, or software language, or cost, etc. You can segment computer users on the basis of financial business users, scientist business users, game recreational users, students, writers, etc. A high-speed high memory capacity computer involving complicated software and a high price might be right for a research scientist, but it wouldn't be a good fit for a home student application. A relatively inexpensive and much easier to use computer will be of interest to the student but not to the scientist.

A full segmentation scheme for the above would be a two dimensional matrix with computer attributes on one axis and user characteristics on the other axis. Each matrix cell represents a potential market segment. Some cells are not attractive segments, such as the intersection of high school students with a million dollar super computer. The market size is not worth pursuing. Some cells are legitimate segments, such as research

P	C1P1	C2P1	C3P1
R			
O	C1P2	C2P2	C3P2
D			
U	C1P3	C2P3	C3P3
C			
T	C1P4	C2P4	C3P4

Segmentation Matrix Example

scientists with the same super computer. But, you may choose not to participate because you don't have the technological expertise to design and build such computers. Other cells may be exactly what you want, such as recreational users with moderate cost computers because you are good at writing game software.

Many other attributes can be assigned to segments, or sometimes, subsegments. Geography, age, occupation, place or time of use, life-style, personality, sex, pioneer innovators, long-term loyal users, financial condition, specific benefits sought, etc.

With the above in mind consider the following respecting market segments involving your product(s).

1. Identify and describe the attributes of the market segment(s) at which you aim your product.

2. Show a complete market segmentation into which this segment fits, such as the customer and product matrix above.

3. Identify cells which do not form useful segments for anybody (per high school student with super computer example). Of the remaining segments, identify those in which you compete with this product or a minor variation of it. Identify segments in which you compete with other products. Identify segments in which you don't compete.

4. Do segment cells in which you compete form a pattern? You offer all the product versions a particular customer segment wants if you compete across a full vertical column, such as all the C2 cells. While you are focused on making your product meet all customer needs if you compete across a horizontal row such as all P1 cells.

5. Knowing what you know of the market, your products, your objectives, your capabilities, etc., is there a desired or optimum segment cell pattern you ought to address? What are you missing? What will it take to get there?

6. Is your business structure involving sales, manufacturing, etc. appropriate for the market address pattern you found? Should you change your organizational focus to better compete in the areas you have chosen? Should you change your market focus to better fit your structure?

7. Examine the customer attributes for the various cells. Are they well and completely described. Are these indeed unique segments? Should some be further segmented into sub-segments? Can some segments be merged?

8. Consider the price implications of your segment mix. Does it make sense, for instance, to compete across three customer segments with the same product at the same price? Is this the right price for the segment(s)? If no, what is the right price? What can/will you do about it (change price, change product, change segments, etc.)?

9. Locate competing products on your segment chart and consider whether you like what you see. What can/will you do if you aren't happy with the competitive situation?

10. Provide market size and growth estimates for the total market and individual segments. Are you missing from some attractive segment(s)? Why are you not there? What will it take to be there?

7.6 P-V results

Price affects sales volume quantity. Price and units volume together determine sales revenue and profit or loss results. Hence, you need to consider volume whenever you consider price in order to determine the impact on your business.

Provide price-demand information for your product(s) by filling out the form below. The upper part is in currency units (such as dollars) while the lower part is in percentage of current position. Choose whatever price change increments and range you find useful. A minimal exercise involves 5% change increments at 20% total change in price, up and down. Extend the information as much as you can in both directions if at

Price = P, Units quantity = Q, Sales Revenue = QP, Cost = C, Contribution to profit = Q (P − C)

Price ($)									
Units									
Revenue									
Contribution									

NOW

Price (%)				100					
Units (%)				100					
Revenue				100					
Contribution									

P-V Analysis Form

all possible. The contribution to profit result involves taking into account a "cost" component. This is usually taken to be the total product related variable cost or the manufacturing variable cost. But you can use whatever is needed for your situation, including fully absorbed allocated cost.

Accurate demand curve information is very difficult to obtain. Hence, it may be necessary to perform this exercise three times: Once at the upper quantity expectation for the price, once at the lower quantity possibility, and once at the most likely.

1. At what prices are the revenue and contribution maxima? You will need to extend the demand information range beyond your original if you have not reached these maxima.

2. Is the current price where you want to be in view of prices that yield maximum sales and maximum contribution?

3. How sure are you of the "most likely" demand results? How much do prices for maximum sales and maximum revenue move when you use the upper and lower volume demand projections? Do you have useful information here or do you need to determine more accurate demand information?

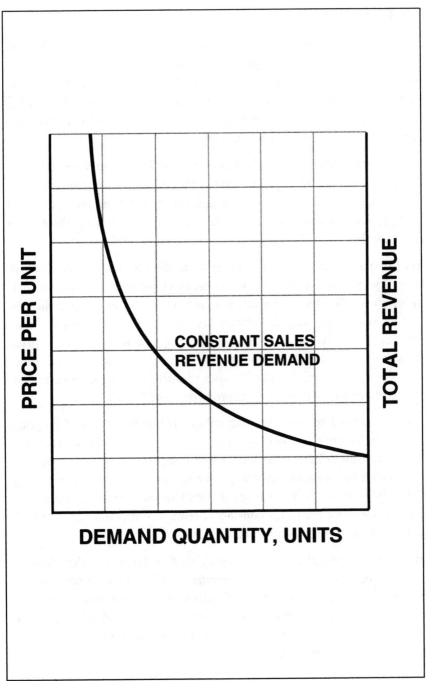

Figure 7.1. Price-Demand Graph.

7.7 P-V graph

Figure 7.1 is a copy of figure 3.4 showing a constant-revenue demand curve. You will find this graph shown in two ways in the literature, with ordinate and abscissa axes interchanged. I prefer the price and revenue result on the vertical, as in figure 7.1, though I did it the other way for mathematical convenience in figure 6.1. Take care not to confuse one arrangement with the other when using other references.

The constant-revenue graph is a good starting point when doing a demand as a function of price analysis. Plot your demand data on a copy of 7.1, or construct your own constant revenue P-V graph. A constant revenue result means that the product of price and units quantity is a constant, thus QP = R = constant.

Your demand relationship can differ from the constant revenue one in several ways. You could cross the constant curve with a steeper or shallower slope. The former indicates a less elastic demand, while the former shows a more elastic demand. See figure 3.5 for examples. Less elasticity indicates that volume is less dependent on price. A price change will not affect volume very much. Hence, assuming that other considerations permit it, it's desirable to operate at the high price end. Do you have an opportunity to improve business results here?

A more elastic demand means that volume is highly influenced by price. A small price change will result in a large change in volume. Your best business result will be at the high volume end. Here you have to look at manufacturing capacity and competitor response to aggressive pricing. Other P-V shapes provide more difficult to interpret implications. A curve completely above the constant revenue result is indicative of multiple segment commingling as shown in figure 5.1.

In addition to considering your most likely P-V graph, it's also useful to compare results against the high volume and low volume possibilities. The spread of these curves is indicative of your level of uncertainty about the P-V data. A wide spread means a high level of uncertainty. This may call for contingency plans so you have a safe landing option if things don't go as planned.

7.8 Contribution to profit

Deducting product-related costs from revenue yields contribution to profit. I usually identify the variable cost explicitly as VC, but sometimes use C when speaking in general terms. Ideally these costs are directly connected to, and vary with, the product. Remove the product and you remove this cost. An important point to remember is that it's not possible to recover all of this cost via a price change. You can only recover roughly half of this cost through a price increase. A higher price than that will lose so much volume that the contribution will actually diminish. Hence, it's very important to reduce this cost to a minimum.

Whatever the variable cost may be, there's always a need to find a "best" price. But price affects volume, which together provide a contribution to profit. One way to approach this issue is via a constant contribution analysis. A price change that yields more volume than needed for constant contribution will improve the profit result, while one that yields less volume than needed for constant contribution will diminish the profit result.

Let $P1$ = current price, and $Q1$ is the resulting current unit volume. The cost associated with the product equals C. A change in price to $P2$ will result in a change in volume to $Q2$. For constant contribution to profit we have: $Q1 (P1 - C) = Q2 (P2 - C)$.

The new volume needed to maintain the contribution to profit is given, for example, by:

$$Q2 = Q1 * (P1 - C) / (P2 - C)$$

The product sells for $6,500, volume is 100 (units or thousands of units, or whatever), and the variable cost is $2,600. We reduce the price to $6,175. What volume do we need to achieve so as to not lose contribution to profit?

$$Q2 = 100 * (6,500 - 2,600) / (6,175 - 2,600) = 109$$

We will lose contribution to profit if volume does not increase by 9 out of 100 units, or 9%.

A percent-based calculation is frequently easier to work with than one based on absolute quantities. If we call the price change P% and the cost as a percent of initial price C%, then a bit of manipulation of the constant contribution equation yields:

$$Q2 = Q1 * (C\% - 1) / (C\% - 1 + P\%)$$

For C% = 2,600 / 6,500 = 0.40 and P% = (6,500 – 6,175) / 6,500 = 0.05:

$$Q2 = 100 * (0.4 - 1) / (0.4 - 1 + 0.05) = 109.$$

Now you can use the percentage demand information from 7.6 to check whether a price change will improve or reduce profits.

An alternative procedure is to use a graph as given in figure 7.2. This shows a family of two constant contribution curves at variable cost of 10% and 50% of the initial (100%) price. Thus, for a 10% variable cost, the contribution to profit at the 100% (current) point is 100 (100 – 10) = 9,000. At a price of 60%, we have 180% units and the contribution to profit is still 9,000, (180 (60 –10) = 9,000). At a price of 110% the units quantity is decreased to 90 and the contribution is again 90 (110 – 10) = 9,000.

Some people prefer to use a table to check on price change results. Two such tables, one for a price increase and one for a price reduction, are provided below.

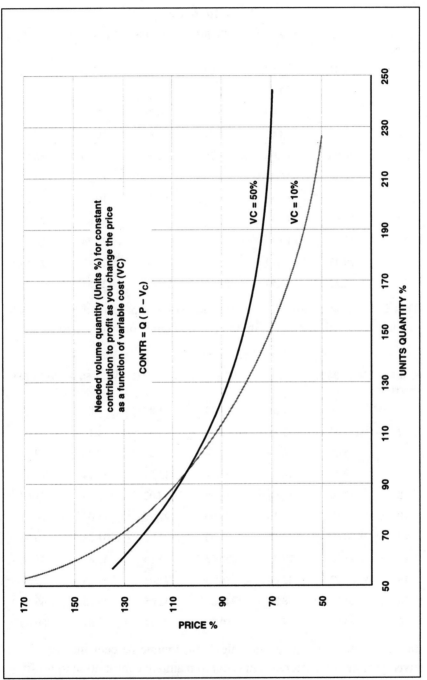

Figure 7.2. Contribution to Profit Pricing.

Price Increase

% price increase	VC = 30%	VC = 35%	VC = 40%	VC = 45%	VC = 50%	VC = 55%
1	1.41	1.52	1.64	1.79	1.96	2.17
2	2.78	2.99	3.23	5.51	3.85	4.26
4	5.41	5.80	6.25	6.78	7.41	8.16
6	7.89	8.45	9.09	9.84	10.71	11.76
8	10.26	10.96	11.76	12.70	13.79	15.09
10	12.50	13.33	14.29	15.38	16.67	18.18
12	14.63	15.58	16.67	17.91	19.35	21.05
14	16.67	17.72	18.92	20.29	21.88	23.73
16	18.60	19.75	21.05	22.54	24.24	26.23
18	20.45	21.69	23.08	24.66	26.47	28.57
20	22.22	23.53	25.00	26.67	28.57	30.77

This is the maximum permissible unit volume percent decrease for a given percent price increase in order to maintain contribution to profit.

Price Decrease

% price decrease	VC = 30%	VC = 35%	VC = 40%	VC = 45%	VC = 50%	VC = 55%
1	1.45	1.56	1.69	1.85	2.04	2.27
2	2.94	3.17	3.45	4.65	4.17	4.65
4	6.06	6.56	7.14	7.84	8.70	9.76
6	9.38	10.17	11.11	12.24	13.64	15.38
8	12.90	14.04	15.38	17.02	19.05	21.62
10	16.67	18.18	20.00	22.22	25.00	28.57
12	20.69	22.64	25.00	27.91	31.58	36.36
14	25.00	27.45	30.43	34.15	38.89	45.16
16	29.63	32.65	36.36	41.03	47.06	55.17
18	34.62	38.30	42.86	48.65	56.25	66.67
20	40.00	44.44	50.00	57.14	66.67	80.00

This is the minimum required sales unit volume percent increase for a given percent price decrease in order to maintain contribution to profit.

7.9 Break-even analysis

A contribution to profit as discussed in 7.8 is not the same as profit. You will end at a loss if the contribution to profit is not sufficient to cover your fixed costs (FC). You need sufficient unit volume (Q) to at least break-even. Otherwise your business is losing money. Do either a graphical B-E analysis per figure 3.7, or compute the B-E quantity volume from: $Q = FC / (P - VC)$. If you have an earnings target (E), then the units quantity is increased to $Q = (FC + E) / (P - VC)$.

1. How does the above compare to your P-V results?

2. Do you need to improve?

3. You can try for more price, more volume, less fixed cost, or less variable cost. The most effective is a cost reduction because the savings flow straight to the bottom line. In any event. What are your action items? What will you do? When and who will do it? What are the strategic consequences? Etc.

7.10 Operating efficiency

How efficiently you use your labor and assets will determine your cost basis and profit. A lower cost permits a lower price which yields more volume and more profit. Furthermore, the rate of return of operating income on assets is an important measure of profit. Return on assets is the ratio of earnings to assets, $ROA = E / A$. This is the same as the product of asset turns, $T = Sales / A$, times percent earnings margin, $M = E / Sales$. The same ROA can be obtained at different combinations of percent margin (M), and asset turns (T). Figure 7.3 shows a family of constant ROA lines using different profit and turn values. How you make your investment decisions respecting use of equipment versus labor, efficiency with which you use your invested capital and capacity utilization level all determine your operating choice and how efficiently you carry it out.

1. Place an O on figure 7.3 at your earnings, turns, and ROA objectives.

2. Place an R on figure 7.3 at the actual results.

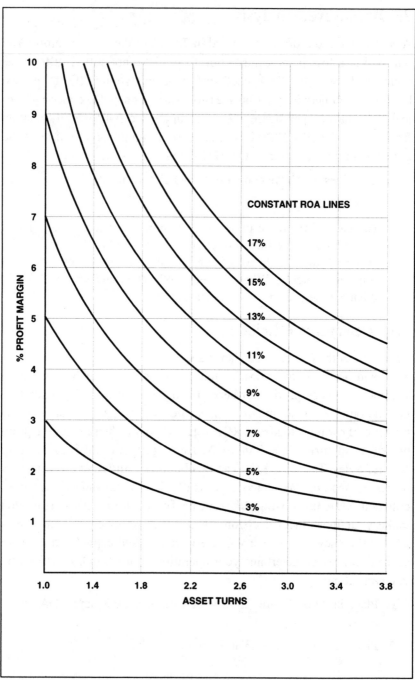

Figure 7.3. Return on Assets Relationships.

3. Does the result fall short of target? What will/can you do to move turns and margins to the target line? Frequently, it's taken that you need higher asset turns to improve ROA. But this need not be so. Remember that ROA is not a point, but a line. Can you possibly trade between turns and margin to get there?

The most efficient operating asset utilization is obtained at full capacity. That's why it can be worthwhile to use an incremental sales strategy to get full capacity utilization, even when that reduces the profit margin. But you have to be careful in how you define the word "full". Try to go too full and you could look like a fool. Machinery wears out when you run it 24 hours a day without stop. You need maintenance stops. You may also need some safety for scheduling or parts availability time loss. Full capacity is not necessarily 100% equipment and time use.

Furthermore, the marginal labor cost will increase as you get closer to the 100% point due to the need to ensure that all process aspects are perfectly timed and executed. A higher labor cost means less margin and less ROA. Generally, though, one can trade labor cost, and margin erosion, for asset cost and turns erosion. Therefore, there is a range of labor and asset costs that yield a relatively equal full capacity result. This is illustrated in figure 7.4. The concept behind figure 7.4 is simple. But getting real numbers for a real situation is very difficult. Hence, labor vs asset investment decisions are usually made on a case-by-case basis and with insufficient trade-off information. It's important, though, to understand that such a relationship does exist. You make a strategic investment and long-term business direction decision every time you hire a person or buy an asset.

7.11 Profit, price, and value

Everybody knows that you can't stay in business while losing money. Many people think that all is well, however, if you make a "profit". More profit will make you richer, and less profit will make you not so rich. But all is well as long as there's a profit. But it takes more than breaking even to survive into the future. Indeed, some management thinkers would like to eliminate the word "profit" altogether as misleading into a false sense of security. The position is that what we call profit is simply a current surplus that the business will need in the future. Peter

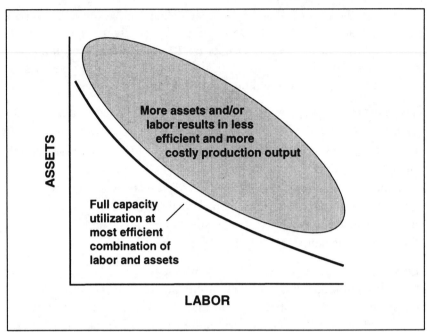

Figure 7.4. Manufacturing Efficiency Relationships.

Drucker calls it, "earning today the cost of staying in business tomorrow". He makes it clear in *Managing in Turbulent Times* that "the cost of staying in business can never be lower than the cost of capital". Therefore, whatever your primary business objective might be, you will not succeed without a reasonable surplus, or "profit" as I call it, to cover the cost of staying in business in the future.

Whether we call it profit or surplus, we are talking about what remains from incoming revenue after you pay your expenses. You can only have a profit if there's incoming revenue. Incoming revenue is the product of units sold and price per unit. But the volume of units sold is connected to price through the P-V demand relationship. Hence, price is a critical driver to profit which is essential for staying in business.

Price, by itself, does not provide income. Only a price that someone pays via a sale provides revenue. And a buyer will only accept a price that provides value. Thus, from 2.3, "Successful pricing must meet the customer's perception of value." This is a difficult area to deal with because there are no clearly quantifiable measures to indicate what the customer values or how well your offering fits in. Even if your product is a perfect fit, it's necessary that the customer "perceive" this. Only value perceived by the customer will influence the sale. The buyer does not pay for your costs, but only for the value you provide. Hence, cost reduces profit. A cost at 50% of maximum price reduces contribution to profit to 25% of what you have at zero cost. A 90% cost component yields only 1% of contribution compared to the ideal zero cost situation as discussed in section 6.5 and illustrated in figure 7.5. You must minimize the cost and maximize the value.

Matching your offering and customer perception of value is a critical factor in business success. This involves a combination of the following:

• Discovering what the customer values. This information is used for new product planning and/or in promoting existing products. Some examples respecting this are provided in 3.19.

• Assigning a customer value to a product(s) is also discussed in 3.19. This information is used for competitive product comparison and competitive price setting.

• An important area, not discussed in this book, involves product promotion, or advertising, to acquaint the customer with product attributes and show that these fit the perceived value profile.

• Finally, we have the inverse of the above where, the promotion aims to shape content of the desired values profile in order to shift the perceived desires towards the product offering.

Ultimately, a potential customer makes a decision to buy or not to buy on the basis of perceived product value and fit of price to this value and competitive product value. This is the decision factor that's used in price-gap analysis. Try to answer the following questions as best you can, and consider what it would take to find answers to those questions that you can't now answer.

• Who is the customer (segment)?

• Describe the customer segment in terms of distinguishing attributes that make this group a distinct segment compared to other user groups.

• What does this segment value?

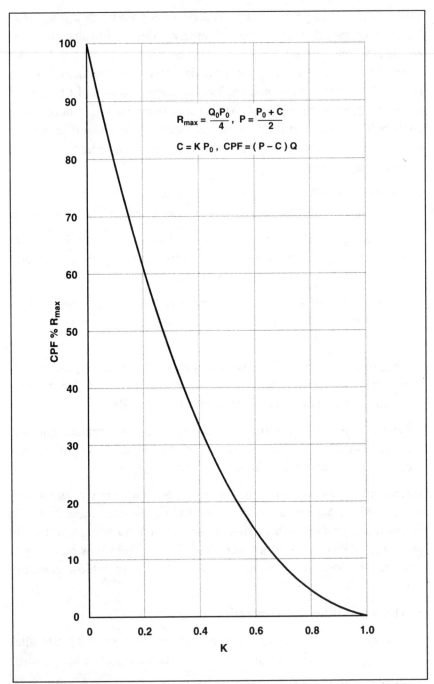

Figure 7.5. Cost Impact on Profit.

Appendix

- How well does your product meet the value profile? We are good or we are not good is not sufficient. Be specific.

- What is the customer's perception of the value of your offering? Does the customer know about your product?

- Do you need or want to change something? E.g., the product attributes, the customer segment, customer perception of what you offer, customer perception of what to value, etc.

- Devise an action plan that is within your resource means to carry out to achieve the desired changes.

- Add to the above a comparison to your internal objectives and position the product on a price gap matrix.

- Do you need to make changes?

- Devise a plan that is realistically within your means to carry out.

7.12 About strategic behavior

Strategic behavior consists of three basic components:

- Goals, objectives, convictions, beliefs, intentions... This area is frequently neglected as not being amenable to analytic or mathematical analysis. The subject is frequently disparaged as belonging to the "soft", or "touchy-feely" part of business and not worthy of attention by hard-headed business people. Neglect of this area can be costly. Many otherwise brilliant plans frequently fail as a consequence. This is because the real world seldom cooperates to meet a set up scenario. The real world is a hard place that refuses to do your bidding. It takes hard work, it takes perseverance, and above all, it takes conviction to get something done. And conviction comes from a strong core set of beliefs and objectives. Why continue on a difficult road if you are not convinced that the "rainbow" is at the end of the road and it's a worthy objective to work for? Certainly, conviction must be tested by analysis for real possibility. Wanting the impossible will not get it for you no matter how hard you try. But it's well established that a less "competent" champion will succeed more frequently than a presumably more competent disinterested party. You must know what your beliefs, intentions, and objectives are, if you are to succeed at strategic behavior. The above is summarized in section 2.1 by the statement that: "Above all, the critical questions are human questions to be answered by people and not equations. Why are you in business? What are your business objectives? What are your profit objectives? How do you want to treat people (employees, customers, competitors...)? These are matters that cannot be answered by a price-demand curve. Once you've answered these questions, however, analysis will help you achieve the results you're after."

- Strategies, tactics, and all the accompanying analyses of markets, competitors, costs, resources, capabilities, etc., forms the usual subject matter of a typical strategic plan. Part of this plan usually contains a section on action items. What is to be done? Who will do it? How much will it cost? How long will it take? Etc. Sometimes this is appended to the strategic plan as a separate document. In any event, it's a necessary part of the planning process and is usually done pretty well. But planning is not the end intent of the process.

- The end intent of strategic behavior is to get something accomplished. This means that you must do something, and do it successfully. This is an area where well-conceived plans frequently fall apart.

With the above in mind, I suggest that you deal directly, and separately, with the following items no matter what sort of strategic plan you prepare.

- What is the single most important critical factor of success in your business? What are the practical, action oriented, elements that you have implemented, or are implementing, to succeed at this critical factor? Be specific, quantifiable (where possible), brief, and speak in plain language.

- Explain in one paragraph what you are trying to achieve. No special technical terminology or jargon please.

- What are the obstacles to success? How will these be overcome?. What resources will it take? How sure are you of success if you get these resources?

- What difference will it make (identify to whom — you, business, etc.) if you do succeed?

- How long to a first result? How long to a final result?

- How will you test for progress? Provide quantifiable measures.

- Under what conditions will this project be terminated?

- Will somebody want to buy this thing at a price that we can afford to sell? Who will buy?

- Do we have the people skills, plant and equipment resources, financial resources, etc., to develop, build, and sell this item?

- Do we know how to build it in quantity, at an acceptable price, and quality?

- What will the competition do?

7.13 Quotable quotes

- The ultimate objective of every business manager, no matter what the function or management designation, should be to aim for overall business success.

- Analysis is no substitute for thinking. Compare analysis to practical experience.

- The critical questions are human questions to be answered by people and not equations.

- Successful pricing must meet the customer's perception of value.

- The buyer's needs, wants, financial condition, competitive offerings, seller's offering all contribute to perception of value.

- The price-to-the-user is not necessarily the same as the income-to-the-seller. You must determine the true cost and not just the base sales price when comparing value against competitive products.

- Cost control is a critical factor in pricing strategy. Any cost increase must increase the value to the customer so as to improve the P-V demand position. Otherwise, profit will suffer.

- A market segment involves a subset of customers who value substantially similar product or service parameters, and whose interests and/or needs and/or values differ sufficiently from others to be differentiated and treated differently.

- Choose the segments for your business, or overall market, on the basis of externals:Customer interests or needs. Competitor behavior or offerings. The world economic or political situation. Etc.

- Choose which segments to compete in or emphasize on the basis of internals: What are your strengths? Where can you make a difference. What are your interests? Where can you win? Etc.

- A want or need or desire for the product, knowledge and appreciation of the value of the product, and financial ability to pay for the product, describes a desirable customer.

- Winning behavior results from planning + thinking + action. Such behavior is strategic. The aim of strategic behavior is to achieve results which are representative of business success.

7.14 Discounted net present value

The net present value of $1 discounted at i% for n periods is:

$$NPV = 1 / (1 + i)^n$$

n	4%	5%	6%	8%	10%	12%	14%	16%	18%	20%
1	0.962	0.952	0.943	0.926	0.909	0.893	0.877	0.862	0.847	0.833
2	0.925	0.907	0.890	0.857	0.826	0.797	0.769	0.743	0.718	0.694
3	0.889	0.864	0.840	0.794	0.751	0.712	0.675	0.641	0.609	0.579
4	0.855	0.823	0.792	0.735	0.683	0.636	0.592	0.552	0.516	0.482
5	0.822	0.784	0.747	0.681	0.621	0.567	0.519	0.476	0.437	0.402
6	0.790	0.746	0.705	0.630	0.564	0.507	0.456	0.410	0.370	0.335
7	0.760	0.711	0.665	0.583	0.513	0.452	0.400	0.354	0.314	0.279
8	0.731	0.677	0.627	0.540	0.467	0.404	0.351	0.305	0.266	0.233
9	0.703	0.645	0.592	0.500	0.424	0.361	0.308	0.263	0.225	0.194
10	0.676	0.614	0.558	0.463	0.386	0.322	0.270	0.227	0.191	0.162
11	0.650	0.585	0.527	0.429	0.350	0.287	0.237	0.195	0.162	0.135
12	0.625	0.557	0.497	0.397	0.319	0.257	0.208	0.168	0.137	0.112
13	0.601	0.530	0.469	0.368	0.290	0.229	0.182	0.145	0.116	0.093
14	0.577	0.505	0.442	0.340	0.263	0.205	0.160	0.125	0.099	0.062
15	0.555	0.481	0.417	0.315	0.239	0.183	0.140	0.108	0.084	0.065
16	0.534	0.458	0.394	0.292	0.218	0.163	0.123	0.093	0.071	0.054
17	0.513	0.436	0.317	0.270	0.198	0.146	0.108	0.080	0.060	0.045
18	0.494	0.416	0.350	0.250	0.180	0.130	0.095	0.069	0.051	0.038
19	0.475	0.396	0.331	0.232	0.164	0.116	0.083	0.060	0.043	0.031
20	0.456	0.377	0.312	0.215	0.149	0.104	0.073	0.051	0.037	0.026

7.15 Definitions

Accounts payable — money you owe to suppliers.

Accounts receivable — money customers owe you.

Accrual accounting — revenue and expenses are recognized when transacted, rather than when cash is received or paid.

Allocated costing — costs are assigned or allocated to products or departments based on an allocation scheme or formula.

Assets — economic resources, such as cash or machinery, owned by the business.

Asset turnover ratio — measure of asset utilization efficiency. Defined as ratio of sales to assets.

Break-even — sales or unit level at which the business breaks even at zero profit.

CAGR — compound annualized growth rate.

Capital — generally, the monetary value invested in a venture or business.

Capital turnover ratio — revenue divided by invested capital.

Cash accounting — revenue and expenses are recognized when cash is exchanged at payment time.

Cash flow — the amount of cash generated or consumed by a business or activity over a specified time period.

Contribution to profit (also gross profit) — excess of revenue over cost of goods sold (usually variable cost of goods).

Cost — the amount paid by the buyer (see price).

Cost of goods sold (also cost of sales) — total cost involved in acquisition and preparation of goods for sale.

Demand (demand on manufacturing) — product orders.

Discount rate — interest rate used to calculate the present value of future income.

Discounted cash flow — cash flow computed on a discount rate basis.

Earnings (also income and profit) — the excess of revenue over expenses for a specified time period.

Experience curve — showing cost reduction as a function of quantity produced.

Finished goods inventory — built products waiting to be sold.

Fixed cost — a cost that, for a given time period, doesn't change regardless of sales or manufacturing output rate.

Gross margin (also gross profit, also contribution to profit) — excess of sales revenue over cost of goods sold.

Gross margin percentage — gross margin as a percentage of sales revenue.

Gross profit — excess of sales revenue over total cost of inventories sold.

Hurdle rate (also required rate of return) — minimum acceptable return on an investment.

Income (also earnings, profit) — the excess of revenue over expenses.

Income percentage of revenue — income stated as a percentage of revenue; i.e., income divided by revenue.

Income statement (also profit and loss statement) — a report involving revenue, associated expenses, and resulting income over a period of time.

Internal rate of return — the discount rate at which the net present value is zero.

Net income — earnings.

Net present value — current value of future income calculated on a discounted basis.

Net sales — total sales less offsets such as discounts.

Order (also purchase order) — an instruction by buyer to seller to supply, or sell, something.

Payback period — the time it takes to recoup the investment cost.

Present value — the present worth of a future income.

Price — the amount asked by the seller (see cost).

Price-demand graph — same as P-V chart.

Profit margin (also income percentage) — profit expressed as a percent of sales revenue (usually net sales); i.e. income divided by sales.

Profits — excess of revenue over expenses.

P-V chart — a graph showing the relationship between sales, or orders, volume and prices; also income vs volume.

Rate of return — a general term indicating the yield obtained on an asset.

Return on assets — measure of productivity of assets, income as a percent of assets; i.e. income divided by assets.

Return on invested capital — earnings as a percentage of invested capital.

Return on investment — general measure of productivity, earnings on investment as a percentage of investment (e.g., return on assets).

Revenues — sales.

Sale — an exchange or transfer of a good or service for money.

Segments (also market or strategic segments) — a group of customers with similar needs, interests, values.

Sensitivity analysis — analysis of impact on planned result as a function of change of a chosen variable.

Sustainable growth rate — the rate of growth a company can finance from internal cash flow without external borrowing.

Transfer price — the amount charged for a good or service by one subunit of an organization to another subunit of the organization.

Unfilled demand — product orders waiting to be filled (shipped to customer to turn order into sale).

Variable cost — a uniform cost per unit that varies in proportion to total units provided.

Working capital — the excess of current assets over current liabilities.

Zero-sum market — total market sales revenue doesn't change.

7.16 Formulas and symbols

- Assets

  A

- Asset turns ratio

  AT = sales / assets

- Break-even quantity

  $Q_{be} = FC / (P - VC)$

- Contribution to profit

  $CPF = CT = (P - C) Q$, $CT = (P - VC) Q$

- Cost recovery with price increase

  $C / 2$

- Cost (usually variable)

  C, VC

- Demand on manufacturing

  D

- Earnings

  $E = Q (P - VCOS - OVC) - FC$

- Elasticity of demand

  ED = (%change Q) / (%change P)

- Finished goods inventory

  FGI

- Fixed cost

  FC

- Income before tax

  $IBT = SR - $ expense $= CT - FC =$ net $S (1 - \%VCOS - \%OVC) - FC$

- Manufacturing output

  O

- Maximum contribution price

  $P_{max} = (P_0 + VC) / 2$

- Maximum revenue price for straight line P-V

  $P_0 / 2$

- Net present value

  NPV = present value of cash in, minus present value of cash out

- Other variable costs

  OVC

- Payback period

  investment / period income

- Price

  P

- Production output

  O

- Profit

  PF

- Quantity, units volume

  Q, V

- Return on assets $(X = A)$

  $ROA = E / A = \%\text{ profit} * AT$

- Return on X

  $ROX = E / X = \%E / (\text{turns of } X) = E / S * S / X$

- Revenue, sales revenue, sales

  $R = SR = S = Q * P$

- Sum of total assets

  $A_t = A_1 + A_2 + A_3$

- Sum of asset turns ratios

  $1 / AT_t = 1 / AT_1 + 1 / AT_2 + 1 / AT_3$

- Sustainable, self-funded growth at no borrowing and no dividend

  $$\frac{\%\text{Profit}}{[\% (\text{assets} / \text{sales}) - \%\text{ Profit}]}$$

- Transfer price

  TR

- Variable cost

  VC

- Variable cost of sales

  $VCOS$

- Volume for constant contribution to profit with price change

  $Q_2 = Q_1 * (P_1 - C) / (P2 - C)$

  $Q_2 = Q_1 * (\% C - 1) / (\% C - 1 + \% P)$

- Zero volume straight line P-V intercept

  P_0

Index

A

Absorption accounting example, 43

Accounting rate of return, 166

Accrual accounting, 148-149, 164, 167, 206

Aging market, 170

Analysis...
And experience, 19
And results, 19
And thinking, 19, 203

Assumptions, 36, 91, 123, 131, 139

Authority, 75-76

B

Backlog, 161

Behavior, 14, 17, 22, 51, 58, 64, 66-68, 73-74, 76-78, 80-84, 86, 88, 90, 92, 94, 96, 98, 104, 115-118, 136-137, 140, 145, 147, 168-170, 177, 201-202, 204

Bet-your-business, 94

Bidding, 34, 68, 183

Break-even, 14, 30-31, 45-46, 95, 113, 129-130, 138, 195, 206, 210

Break-even analysis, 45

Budget, 91, 151-152

Budgeted, 151

Bundling, 71, 115, 121

Business success, 1, 74, 203

Business definition, 15, 22, 55, 102,

Buy, 5-8, 11, 21, 36, 52, 61, 69, 97, 110, 118-119, 122, 124, 176, 197, 199, 203

Buyer, 2, 6-11, 14, 17, 20-21, 24, 51, 56, 93, 104, 105, 182, 198-199, 203, 206-207

C

Capacity utilization, 14

Cash flow, ii, 165

Commodities, 10, 126

Commodity, 10, 34, 70-71, 126, 183

Competing, 22-23, 28, 38, 47, 54, 57-59, 62, 66, 94, 100-101, 104, 114, 124, 135, 177, 180, 187

D

Demand, 12, 15-16, 21, 25, 28, 31, 34-35, 38, 40-42, 46, 53, 62, 108-111, 113-115, 118, 121-123, 127-131, 133, 136-145, 147, 158-161, 163, 168, 177, 188, 190, 192, 198, 203, 206, 208, 210

Demand...
Analysis, 31
Delivery time strategies, 144
Output capacity strategy, 144
Relationships, 127
Versus delivery time, 141

Versus demo unit level, 141
With break-even, 129
With experience curve, 130

Definition of terms, 206

Demo-demand, 142

Depreciation, 151, 166-167

Direct costing example, 44

Differentiation, 10, 79, 94, 103, 124, 126, 169

Discounted NPV tables, 205

Distribution, 24, 51, 53, 71, 105, 138, 149, 151, 161, 182

Distributor, 27, 86, 151, 161

Drucker, 80, 92, 198

E

Earnings, 11, 63, 65, 148, 150, 152-153, 155, 162, 164-166, 168, 195, 207-208, 210

Economic, 51, 95, 164, 204, 206

Economy, 56, 66, 91

Elasticity (of demand), 35-36, 177, 190, 210

Emerging market, 170

Established market entering, 145

Expense analysis, 152

Experience curve, 46, 63, 113

F

Financial analysis, 79

Financial objectives setting, 174

Foreign sales, 152, 162

Formulas, 12, 127, 154, 161, 171, 210

Future, 2, 9-11, 13, 17, 24, 33, 48-50, 54-56, 63-66, 69, 73, 77-78, 82-83, 86, 88, 90-91, 95, 104-106, 108, 113-115, 161, 166-167, 171, 176-177, 183, 197-198, 206-208

Future...
Forecasting, 82
Predicting, 82

G

Goal, 3, 53, 64, 76, 78-79, 95-96, 116, 201

Growth, 1, 23, 34, 55-56, 63-64, 66-67, 69-70, 74, 85-87, 95-96, 103, 106-107, 115, 145, 162, 165, 168-172, 182-183, 187, 206, 208, 211

Growth, limits to, 171

Growth, sustainable rate, 64

H

Handbook of Business Formulas, 161

Higgins, 64

I

Ideal price, 23

Incentive, 128, 146-147, 152

Income, 4, 21, 30, 64-65, 75, 89, 92, 96, 112, 126, 138, 148-150, 152-153, 156, 161, 164-168, 195, 198, 206-208, 210

Income before tax and fixed cost, 157

Income statement, 149

Incremental sales, 14, 48, 66

Inelastic, 36, 118, 137, 139-140

Inflation, 33, 48-49, 56, 64-66, 105, 167, 182-183

Interdisciplinary, 5

Inter-functional understanding, 5

Internal rate of return, 167

International pricing, 161

Intra-company, 148

Intra-divisional, 148

Intuition, 20, 83, 98

L

Language jargon, 96

Life-cycle, 3, 169-170

Long-range, 83

M

Manager...
  Ultimate objective of, 1

Management obligations, 75

Manufacturing relationships, 157
  Example calculations, 160
  Orders, sales, finished goods relationships, 159

Market environment, 55, 104

Market segmentation, 50, 105

Market segments matrix, 186

Market share, 78, 95
  With competition, 136

Market stability, 67

Matrix strategies, 169

Market structure change, 94

Marketing agents, 87

Money, 6, 11, 28-29, 43-44, 47,
49, 65, 67, 71, 76, 89, 95,
115, 117-118, 120, 126,
148, 154, 156, 166, 168,
177, 195, 197, 206, 208

N

Necessity, 119

Net present value (NPV), 65,
166-167, 205, 207, 210

New competitor, 67, 116

New product, 65

O

Objective...
Primary, 76
Relation to strategy, 76

Objectives, setting, 83

Ohmae, 80, 93

Operating efficiency, 195

Orders-on-hand, 158

Organizational functions...
Interface of, 2, 4

Other product line issues, 61

P

Payback-period, 61, 64, 166

Perceived value, 16

Plan, 10, 13, 30, 66, 74-85, 87-
93, 95, 116, 145, 152,
170, 172-174, 201-202

Plan...
Building, 83
Content and structure, 87
Conventional, 91
Functional, 84
Fit to need, 84
Long and short range, 84

Portfolio, 84
Process, 87
Strategic, 84
Structure examples, 90
Tactical, 84
Users, 88
Who should prepare, 85

Planning, 5, 17, 73-74, 76-77, 79,
81-83, 85, 87, 92-93, 95,
99-100, 102, 104, 106,
108, 110, 112, 114, 116,
118, 120, 122, 124, 126,
145, 169, 173, 199, 202,
204

Planning...
Guidelines, 92

Porter, 80, 90, 93

Power, 75

Portfolio management, 170

Price, 1-18, 20-31, 33-36, 38-42,
46-56, 58-70, 78, 82, 86,
92-93, 96-97, 99-104,
106-111, 113, 115-141,
143, 145, 147-148, 150,
152-154, 161-164, 168-
170, 174-177, 180-185,
187-188, 190-192, 194-
195, 197-199, 201, 203,
206, 208, 210-211

Q

R

Rate-of-return, 166

Rate of return on investment, 93, 95

Re-segmentation, 56, 67, 69, 71, 106, 115, 121

Receivable, 166, 206

Receivables, 50, 155, 168

Resource elements, 92

Return on assets, 1, 145, 155, 176, 195-196, 208, 210

Return on capital, 89, 154, 167

Revenue, 12-13, 16, 25, 30, 34-40, 42-45, 51, 62-63, 67, 108-111, 113, 115-117, 119-122, 130, 132, 135, 138, 143, 148-149, 152-153, 163, 165, 168, 177, 187-188, 190-191, 198, 206-211

Risk, 75, 89, 97

Rivalry, 56

S

Sale, 6-8, 13-14, 18, 20, 42, 47, 51, 67, 96, 100, 103, 118, 135, 145, 147, 149, 156-159, 162, 164, 168, 170, 198-199, 206, 208

Sales, 1-2, 4, 7, 12-16, 18, 21, 23-24, 28-31, 33-36, 38, 40, 43-44, 46, 48, 51, 54-56, 59-64, 66-67, 69, 74, 77-78, 81, 85-87, 89, 95-96, 103, 106-109, 111-113, 115-122, 126, 129-130, 132, 134-135, 138-141, 143, 145, 148-156, 158-165, 168-170, 172, 175-177, 182-184, 187-188, 194-195, 197, 203, 206-211

Sales...
And income, 21
Gross vs net, 149
Per employee, 86
Revenue, 34

Savings, 11, 13, 16, 62, 92, 117, 121, 130, 166, 195

Scenarios, 27-28, 67, 114, 125, 127, 172, 201

Scheuble, 176

Segmentation, 50, 59, 78-79, 105-106, 110, 114, 133, 185-186

Segmented, 54, 187

Segments, 17, 33, 49-56, 59, 66-67, 70, 77-79, 94, 103, 105-106, 111, 118-119, 121-123, 162, 169-171, 175, 177, 179, 183, 185-187, 190, 199, 201, 204, 208

Segments...
Commingled, 121
Questions, 186

T

Time-to-market, 92

Transaction, 20, 96, 154, 168, 176

Turnover, 206

Turns ratios, 154, 165, 211

U

Unbundling, 50, 71, 115, 121

Uncertainty, 9, 17, 160, 176, 190

V

Value, 6-11, 15-16, 20-26, 28, 31, 33, 40-42, 49-71, 76, 80-81, 90, 93-94, 96, 100-104, 106-107, 110, 114-116, 122-123, 126, 133-134, 145, 147, 160-161, 164, 166-167, 169, 176-177, 180-185, 197-199, 201, 203-208, 210

Value...
And buyer, 7
Perception of, 21, 114, 203

Values, 8, 12-13, 21, 51, 59, 70, 106, 134, 145, 160, 195, 199, 204, 208

Variance, 6, 42, 118

W

Worth, 4-9, 15-16, 19-21, 26, 49-51, 64-65, 76, 88, 97, 129, 144-145, 168, 185, 208

Y

Yield, 12, 16, 25, 30, 35, 43-44, 73, 76, 82, 113, 120-121, 130, 132, 134, 136, 138, 140-141, 144, 152-153, 166-167, 173-174, 188, 191-192, 195, 197, 199, 208

Z

Zero-price, 110

Zero sum market, 22, 67, 69, 137, 209

Zero-volume, 110

Zipf's law, 171